The story of Oedipus, the most meaning-laden of myths, has traveled down through history in many guises and forms. Can any one version claim to be definitive? Lowell Edmunds' authoritative survey takes variation as the force driving the myth's longevity and popularity. Refraining from seeking for an original form, Edmunds relates the changes in content to changes in meaning, eschewing the notion that one particular version of the myth can be set as standard.

Oedipus traverses the long history of the myth, from the earliest, pre-tragic Oedipus through fifth-century tragedy, Rome and the Middle Ages, the Renaissance and the Enlightenment, to Oedipus in the nineteenth and twentieth centuries. In illustrating this long history the book shows, in one perspective, a certain continuity, and, in another, a discontinuity followed by a recovery. The agent of continuity is the Roman Seneca, whose *Oedipus* looked back to Greek models, had some currency in the Middle Ages, found many Renaissance imitators, and still sometimes reappears, as in Ted Hughes' adaptation (1969). But the European Middle Ages, Edmunds shows, mark a striking discontinuity in the tradition: for about a millennium, the Oedipus of Greek tragedy is practically forgotten, not to be rediscovered until the fifteenth and sixteenth centuries. Sophocles' *Oedipus the King* is thereafter destined to become the common text of the Oedipus myth.

Oedipus does what no other volume has done before. It analyzes the long and varied history of the myth from ancient times to the modern day and the broad sweep of media in which it has been represented. Lowell Edmunds' *Oedipus* is truly an indispensable guide to the myth of Oedipus.

Lowell Edmunds is Professor of Classics at Rutgers University and an eminent author and researcher. His most recent publications include *Intertextuality and the Reading of Roman Poetry* (2001) and *Poet, Public and Performance: Essays in Ancient Greek Literature and Literary History* (1997).

GODS AND HEROES OF THE ANCIENT WORLD

Series editor Susan Deacy
Roehampton University

Routledge is pleased to present an exciting new series, Gods and Heroes of the Ancient World. These figures from antiquity are embedded in our culture, many functioning as the source of creative inspiration for poets, novelists, artists, composers and filmmakers. Concerned with their multifaceted aspects within the world of ancient paganism and how and why these figures continue to fascinate, the books provide a route into understanding Greek and Roman polytheism in the 21st century.

These concise and comprehensive guides provide a thorough understanding of each figure, offering the latest in critical research from the leading scholars in the field in an accessible and approachable form, making them ideal for undergraduates in Classics and related disciplines.

Each volume includes illustrations, time charts, family trees and maps where appropriate.

Also available:

Zeus
Ken Dowden

Prometheus
Carol Dougherty

Medea
Emma Griffiths

Dionysos
Richard Seaford

Susan Deacy is Lecturer in Greek History and Literature at Roehampton University. Her main research interests are Greek religion, and gender and sexuality. Publications include the co-edited volumes *Rape in Antiquity* (1997) and *Athena in the Classical World* (2001), and the monograph *A Traitor to Her Sex? Athena the Trickster* (forthcoming).

 # OEDIPUS

Lowell Edmunds

 Routledge
Taylor & Francis Group

LONDON AND NEW YORK

First published in the USA and Canada in 2006
by Routledge
270 Madison Avenue, New York, NY 10016

Simultaneously published in the UK
by Routledge
2 Park Square, Milton Park, Abingdon, Oxon OX14 4RN

*Routledge is an imprint of the Taylor & Francis Group,
an informa business*

Typeset in Utopia by
Keystroke, 28 High Street, Tettenhall, Wolverhampton
Printed and bound in Great Britain by
TJ International Ltd, Padstow, Cornwall

Library of Congress Cataloging-in-Publication Data
Edmunds, Lowell.
    Oedipus / Lowell Edmunds.
       p. cm.
    Includes bibliographical references and index.
    1. Oedipus (Greek mythology) I. Title.
    BL820.O43E36 2006
    809'.93351—dc22   2006016085

British Library Cataloguing in Publication Data
A catalogue record for this book is available from the British Library

ISBN10: 0–415–32934–5 (hbk)
ISBN10: 0–415–32935–3 (pbk)
ISBN10: 0–203–39135–7 (ebk)

ISBN13: 978–0–415–32934–7 (hbk)
ISBN13: 978–0–415–32935–4 (pbk)
ISBN13: 978–0–203–39135–8 (ebk)

CONTENTS

SERIES FOREWORD

For a person who is about to embark on any serious discourse or task, it is proper to begin first with the gods.

(Demosthenes, *Letters* 1.1)

WHY GODS AND HEROES?

The gods and heroes of classical antiquity are part of our culture. Many function as sources of creative inspiration for poets, novelists, artists, composers, filmmakers and designers. Greek tragedy's enduring appeal has ensured an ongoing familiarity with its protagonists' experiences and sufferings, while the choice of Minerva as the logo of one of the newest British universities, the University of Lincoln, demonstrates the ancient gods' continued emblematic potential. Even the world of management has used them as representatives of different styles: Zeus and the 'club' culture for example, and Apollo and the 'role' culture: see C. Handy, *The Gods of Management: who they are, how they work and why they fail* (London, 1978).

This series is concerned with how and why these figures continue to fascinate and intrigue. But it has another aim too, namely to explore their strangeness. The familiarity of the gods and heroes risks obscuring a vital difference between modern meanings and ancient functions and purpose. With certain exceptions, people today do not worship them, yet to the Greeks and Romans they were real beings in a system comprising literally hundreds of divine powers. These range from the major gods, each of whom was worshipped in many guises via their epithets or 'surnames', to the heroes – deceased individuals associated with local communities – to other figures such as daimons and nymphs. The landscape was dotted with sanctuaries, while natural features such as mountains, trees and rivers were thought to be inhabited by religious beings. Studying ancient paganism involves finding strategies to comprehend a world where everything was, in the often quoted words of Thales, 'full of gods'.

In order to get to grips with this world, it is necessary to set aside our preconceptions of the divine, shaped as they are in large part by Christianised notions of a transcendent, omnipotent God who is morally good. The Greeks and Romans worshipped numerous beings, both male and female, who looked, behaved and suffered like humans, but who, as immortals, were not bound by the human condition. Far from being omnipotent, each had limited powers: even the sovereign, Zeus/Jupiter, shared control of the universe with his brothers Poseidon/Neptune (the sea) and Hades/Pluto (the underworld). Lacking a creed or anything like an organised church, ancient paganism was open to continual reinterpretation, with the result that we should not expect to find figures with a uniform essence. It is common to begin accounts of the pantheon with a list of the major gods and their function(s) (Hephaistos/Vulcan: craft; Aphrodite/Venus: love; and Artemis/Diana: the hunt and so on), but few are this straightforward. Aphrodite, for example, is much more than the goddess of love, vital though that function is. Her epithets include *Hetaira* ('courtesan') and *Porne* ('prostitute'), but also attest roles as varied as patron of the citizen body (*Pandemos*: 'of all the people') and protectress of seafaring (*Euploia, Pontia, Limenia*).

Recognising this diversity, the series consists not of biographies of each god or hero (though such have been attempted in the past), but of investigations into their multifaceted aspects within the complex world of ancient paganism. Its approach has been shaped partly in response to two distinctive patterns in previous research. Until the middle of the twentieth century, scholarship largely took the form of studies of individual gods and heroes. Many works presented a detailed appraisal of such issues as each figure's origins, myth and cult; these include L.R. Farnell's examination of major deities in his *Cults of the Greek States* (5 vols, Oxford, 1896–1909) and A.B. Cook's huge three-volume *Zeus* (Cambridge, 1914–40). Others applied theoretical developments to the study of gods and heroes, notably (and in the closest existing works to a uniform series) K. Kerényi in his investigations of gods as Jungian archetypes, including *Prometheus: archetypal image of human existence* (English trans. London 1963) and *Dionysos: archetypal image of the indestructable life* (English trans. London 1976).

In contrast, under the influence of French structuralism, the later part of the century saw a deliberate shift away from research into particular gods and heroes towards an investigation of the system of which they were part. Fuelled by a conviction that the study of isolated gods could not do justice to the dynamics of ancient religion, the pantheon came to be represented as a logical and coherent network in which the various powers were systematically opposed to one another. In a classic study by J.-P. Vernant, for example, the Greek concept of space was shown to be consecrated through the opposition between Hestia (goddess of the hearth – fixed space) and Hermes (messenger and traveller god – moveable space: Vernant, *Myth and Thought Among the Greeks*, London, 1983, 127–75). The gods as individual entities were far from neglected, however, as may be exemplified by the works by Vernant, and his colleague M. Detienne, on particular deities including Artemis, Dionysos and Apollo: see, most recently, Detienne's *Apollon, le couteau en main: une approche expérimentale du polythéisme grec* (Paris, 1998).

In a sense, this series is seeking a middle ground. While approaching its subjects as unique (if diverse) individuals, it pays attention to their significance as powers within the collectivity of religious beings. *Gods and Heroes of the Ancient World* sheds new light on many of the most important religious beings of classical antiquity; it also provides a route into understanding Greek and Roman polytheism in the twenty-first century.

The series is intended to interest the general reader as well as being geared to the needs of students in a wide range of fields from Greek and Roman religion and mythology, classical literature and anthropology, to Renaissance literature and cultural studies. Each book presents an authoritative, accessible and refreshing account of its subject via three main sections. The introduction brings out what it is about the god or hero that merits particular attention. This is followed by a central section which introduces key themes and ideas, including (to varying degrees) origins, myth, cult and representations in literature and art. Recognising that the heritage of myth is a crucial factor in its continued appeal, the reception of each figure since antiquity forms the subject of the third part of the book. The volumes include illustrations of each god/hero and where appropriate time charts, family trees and maps. An annotated bibliography synthesises past research and indicates useful follow-up reading.

For convenience, the masculine terms 'gods' and 'heroes' have been selected for the series title, although (and with an apology for the male-dominated language), the choice partly reflects ancient usage in that the Greek *theos* ('god') is used of goddesses too. For convenience and consistency, Greek spellings are used for ancient names, except for famous Latinised exceptions, and BC/AD has been selected rather than BCE/CE.

I am indebted to Catherine Bousfield, the editorial assistant until 2004, who (literally) dreamt up the series and whose thoroughness and motivation brought it close to its launch. The hard work and efficiency of her successor, Matthew Gibbons, has overseen its progress to publication, and the classics editor of Routledge, Richard Stoneman, has provided support and expertise throughout. The anonymous readers for each proposal gave frank and helpful advice, while the authors' commitment to advancing scholarship while producing accessible accounts of their designated subjects has made it a pleasure to work with them.

Susan Deacy, Roehampton University, June 2005

LIST OF MAPS

LIST OF MAPS

LIST OF ILLUSTRATIONS

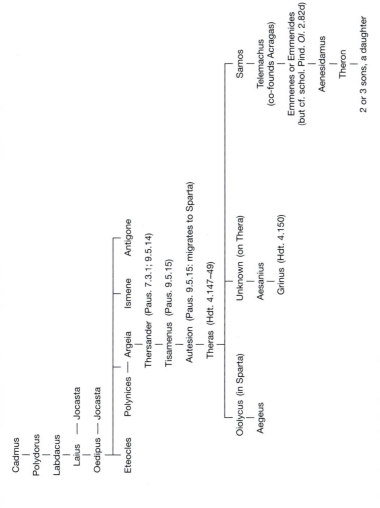

Figure 1 Genealogy of the family of Oedipus.

Greece and Byzantium	Rome	Europe in the Middle Ages and Renaissance
ca. 750–480 BC ARCHAIC PERIOD Oed. in Epic and Lyric	753–31 BC REPUBLIC 753 BC Traditional date of founding of Rome	
480–323 BC CLASSICAL PERIOD Oed. in Tragedy		
323–31 BC HELLENISTIC PERIOD Oed. in Epigram	2nd c. BC Oed. referred to by Plautus and Terence; Theban tragedies of Accius	
31 BC–324 AD ROMAN PERIOD Disappearance of Oed. from Greek literature	31 BC–324 AD HIGH EMPIRE 31 BC–14 AD Augustan poets refer to Oed. 1st c. AD Seneca *Oed. Rex*; Statius *Thebaid*	
325–565 LATE ANTIQUITY Greek literature preserved in the Greek East		325–6th c. LATE ANTIQUITY 5th c. Lactantius Placidus' commentary on Statius[a]
566–1453 BYZANTINE PERIOD		7th c.–13th c. MIDDLE AGES 12th c. *Roman de Thèbes*; *Planctus Oedipi*
		14th c.–15th c. RENAISSANCE Theban myth in Boccaccio (1313–1375) 15th c. Manuscripts of Sophocles reach Italy from Constantinople[b]

Notes

a. 325 AD First Council of Nicaea, convened by Constantine now sole emperor of Eastern Empire, in Bithynia (modern-day Turkey).
566 AD Death of Justinian.

b. 1453 AD Fall of Constantinople to the Turks; beginning of Ottoman period.

Key

→ indicates that there is continuity from the Roman Empire to the European Middle Ages

⋯→ indicates that there is transmission of Oedipus in the Byzantine period directly from the Greek East to Italy

Figure 2 Timeline: the history of the Oedipus myth.

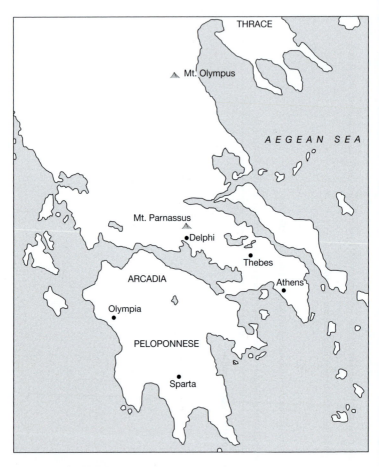

Map 1 Mainland Greece.

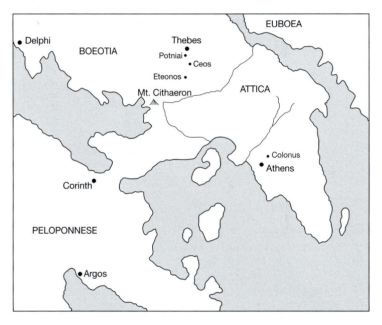

Map 2 Boeotia, Attica, and Northeastern Peloponnese. The exact locations of Ceos and Eteonos are unknown. The locations on this map are approximate.

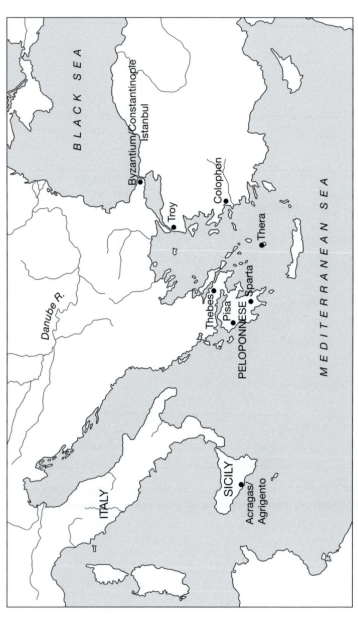

Map 3 Italy, Greece, and Asia Minor.

WHY OEDIPUS?

WHY OEDIPUS?

INTRODUCING OEDIPUS

Don Juan, Don Quixote, Faust, Hamlet, Oedipus – each transcends his national origins and the works of art, music, and literature which have told his story. Each has achieved a special status in the imagination of the West, able to speak powerfully of the human condition. Of the five, Oedipus, once king of Thebes, might claim the largest kingdom in present-day thought.

The particular mode of thought in which he reigns is myth. With apparently inexhaustible capacity for renewal, myth continues to flourish alongside scientific rationality and religion. This mode of thought now has two distinct kinds of expression. One is literary or artistic. The other is intellectual, as thinkers in various fields try to explain the myth's peculiar power. These are the two main kinds of "work on myth," to use Hans Blumenberg's words.[1] This book is about three millennia or so of work on the Oedipus myth.

THE QUESTION OF AN AUTHENTIC VERSION

To retell the myth seems to be the obvious way to start. But the notion of "the" Oedipus myth is precisely the one which this book will put in question. To retell the Oedipus myth is always to retell someone's version and, in so doing, ultimately to give one's own. This point will emerge from Sigmund Freud's summary of Sophocles' *Oedipus the King*, to be quoted below. Freud's work on Oedipus focused on this single tragedy because in his time it had become the basic source for the Oedipus myth. It did not have this status in antiquity, and did not in fact become the common text for the Oedipus myth until the seventeenth century. After Freud, however, the Oedipus Complex and Sophocles' tragedy reaffirm one another in a powerful circle.

It might be thought that, if Sophocles' *Oedipus the King* is going to be ruled out as the authoritative version, one should go back to the earliest version of the Oedipus myth on record. This version will in fact be quoted in the first chapter of this book and will serve as a way of organizing the pre-tragic remains of the myth. Whether the earliest version has any particular right to stand for "the Oedipus myth" is doubtful, however. Found in Homer's *Odyssey*, it has already undergone centuries of work. This epic poem is the end-product of a long tradition, perhaps reaching back into the second millennium BC.

Although this tradition must have had its start-point – one fine day when the first poet chanted the first line of the epic – this premiere began to recede from memory as soon as the second performance began. The "author" (not likely to have been using writing but working orally) disappeared in the tradition as it gathered momentum and proliferated. The poem could not survive if it could not be repeated, and it could not be repeated without adjusting to new circumstances and new audiences, sometimes far from its point of origin (wherever that was). In short, it could not be repeated without variation. Oedipus had his own epic, too, no longer extant, with its own tradition. The ten-line summary of the Oedipus myth in the *Odyssey* is probably the story line of that epic. Already, then, in its earliest recorded form, the Oedipus myth is the product of work on myth, a particular variant, without any rightful claim to stand for "the Oedipus myth."

Variation persists down into the fifth century BC. In his three Theban tragedies, not constituting a trilogy in the ancient sense but written for, and produced on, different occasions, Sophocles is working with slightly different versions of the myth each time. In *Antigone*, Oedipus is already dead and buried in Thebes. In *Oedipus at Colonus*, he dies in the village named in the title, near Athens. At the end of *Oedipus the King*, Oedipus is still alive, and it is not certain whether he will stay in Thebes or go into exile. So even in the fifth century, the Oedipus myth did not have the canonical fixity that one tends to assume that it had.

To bedevil further the question of an authentic version, one has to observe that the Oedipus myth was unlikely to have been the exclusive possession of bards and poetic traditions. No doubt it was told, like many another Greek myth, casually, in prose, as a story for entertainment or admonition, thus in a popular tradition parallel to the poetic one. It can be shown that oral traditions of this kind concerning Oedipus, attached to hero cults honoring him, persisted down into the fifth century BC. (Ch. 2).

If one is not going to talk about an authentic version, how is one going to talk about the myth? The first answer might be: focus on the character of Oedipus. But if one starts from the principle of variation, then the character of Oedipus will be seen to vary, too, on the assumption that the character is the product of the story and not vice versa. This assumption is, in fact, the crucial one that is being made here: there was never, nor is there now, an Oedipus existing apart from the stories told about him, in whatever medium. One needs, then, some other answer than the character of Oedipus to the question of how to talk about the myth, and that answer will be a method borrowed from folklore studies. This method is convenient in the case of Oedipus because his story flourished as a folktale in oral traditions in modern times, and was classified as a type (number 931) in the standard index of folktale types by Antti Aarne and Stith Thompson.[2] Though they named the type "Oedipus" because of its obvious resemblance to the myth, the protagonist of the folktale is not "Oedipus" but usually just "a boy," or, if he has a name, it is "Jack" or the like.

SEGMENTING THE NARRATIVE INTO MOTIFS

The Oedipus type as defined by Aarne and Thompson takes the form of a list of motifs. These are minimal units of the narrative. This simple method of *segmenting the narrative into motifs* greatly facilitates comparison of different folktale versions. It will also prove to be useful for dealing with the variants of the ancient myth and indeed with the whole history of the myth.

For the Oedipus folktale, Aarne and Thompson give:

Parricide prophecy
Mother-incest prophecy
Exposure of child to prevent fulfillment of parricide prophecy
Compassionate executioner
Exposed or abandoned child rescued
Exposed infant raised at strange king's court (Joseph, Oedipus)
Parricide prophecy unwittingly fulfilled
Mother–son incest

These motifs have generic rubrics in the index because they take different, specific forms in different folktales, and different characters can undergo the same experiences (thus "Joseph, Oedipus"). Cross-references (not included here) point to Thompson's *The Motif-Index of Folk-Lore*, where one can see how the same motifs turn up individually in types of folktale other than "Oedipus."

If one wanted to use the list of the generic motifs of the Oedipus folktale diagnostically to construct a list of the motifs of the Oedipus myth in Sophocles' *Oedipus the King*, one would have to define the specific form of these motifs in Sophocles. One would also, however, have to be alert for motifs found in Sophocles but not in Aarne and Thompson's list. Such a list for Sophocles would include the following (motifs not in Aarne and Thompson are indicated by a plus [+] sign):

Parricide prophecy received by Laius, father of Oedipus
Exposure of Oedipus to prevent fulfillment of parricide prophecy
+Mutilation of Oedipus (ankles pierced)
Compassionate executioner (Theban herdsman)
Oedipus rescued by Corinthian herdsman
Oedipus raised by Polybus, king of Corinth
+Oedipus leaves Corinth after taunted as bastard by drunken comrade
Mother-incest prophecy +and parricide prophecy received by Oedipus
Oedipus unwittingly fulfills parricide prophecy
+Oedipus solves riddle of Sphinx and thus slays the monster
Oedipus marries his mother
+Becomes king of Thebes

+Plague in Thebes, initiating quest for murderer of Laius
+He discovers his crimes
+She commits suicide
+He blinds himself

To compare this list with Aarne and Thompson's, the most striking differences are the monster-slaying and the discovery of the crimes, with grisly consequences. Aarne and Thompson probably left the ending of the folktale blank because it varies widely. Their omission of monster-slaying accurately reflects the absence of this motif in folktales of the Oedipus type.[3]

FREUD AND SOPHOCLES

The protagonist's discovery of his crimes of course forms the plot of Sophocles' *Oedipus the King*. The folktale type serves as a reminder that Sophocles has built a tragedy on the elaboration of a single motif. This tragedy is thus a combination of two stories, one about a detective in search of himself, and the other about his discovery of his past, which amounts to what we would call the myth of Oedipus. Though a synopsis of the tragedy and a synopsis of the myth are two different things, it is possible to combine them, as Freud did:

Oedipus, son of Laius, King of Thebes, and of Jocasta, was exposed as an infant because an oracle had warned Laius that the still unborn child would be his father's murderer. The child was rescued, and grew up as a prince in an alien court, until, in doubt as to his origin, he too questioned the oracle and was warned to avoid his home since he was destined to murder his father and take his mother in marriage. On the road leading away from what he believed was his home, he met King Laius and slew him in a sudden quarrel. He came next to Thebes and solved the riddle set him by the Sphinx who barred his way. Out of gratitude the Thebans made him their king and gave him Jocasta's hand in marriage. He reigned long in peace and honour, and she who, unknown to him, was his mother bore him two sons and two daughters. Then at last a plague broke out and the Thebans made enquiry once more of the oracle. It is at this point that Sophocles' tragedy opens. The messengers bring back the reply that the plague will cease

> when the murderer of Laius has been driven from the land. [Here Freud quotes
> lines 108–9 from the play.] The action of the play consists in nothing other than
> the process of revealing, with cunning delays and ever-mounting excitement . . .
> that Oedipus himself is the murderer of Laius, but further that he is the son of the
> murdered man and of Jocasta. Appalled at the abomination which he has
> unwittingly perpetrated, Oedipus blinds himself and forsakes his home. The oracle
> has been fulfilled.[4]

"Warned to avoid his home" is Freud's elaboration of the oracle. The
"messengers" are really only Creon, the brother of Jocasta. But these
are minor errors. Of greater interest is "the Sphinx who barred his
way," a characterization which might imply an "Oedipal" intention on
Oedipus' part to enter the city. Nothing in Sophocles suggests such an
intention. The encounter with the Sphinx receives only brief notice in
the tragedy. Oedipus, one infers, knew the challenge of the riddle
(answer or die) and sought the challenge. Contrary to what Freud
may be implying, Sophocles gives no indication that Oedipus had any
inkling that he would be rewarded by marriage to the widowed queen
of Thebes. One has to assume that, at the time he solved the riddle,
Oedipus did not know of the existence of this widow. In contrast
to Freud's insinuation of something not in the ancient myth stands
his glaring omission of something that few readers or spectators of
Sophocles could forget: the suicide of Jocasta.

Although Freud was a masterthinker of the twentieth century, and
his synopses of myth and tragedy are as good as any that one will find,
they are far from authoritative. Rather, they amount (inevitably, as I
have suggested) to a new variant, influenced by the interpretive stance
of the teller. The outcome of the discovery has relevance in Freud's
mind only for Oedipus, and the suicide of the hero's mother/wife is
of no interest. The life of Oedipus beyond the self-blinding is in fact of
no interest to Freud, whereas it was of tremendous interest through
most of the history of the myth, and, at the time of this writing, the
summer of 2004, *The Gospel at Colonus* – a blues and gospel version of
Sophocles' tragedy on the death of Oedipus – is being performed in
New York.

SCOPE OF THIS BOOK

To remain true to the nature of the evidence, this survey of the Oedipus myth keeps its eye on variations in the story, accepting variation as a driving force, and refrains from looking for an original form of the myth or an "authoritative" version. Changes in the story are of course related to changes in its meaning. If one is going to track open-mindedly the profoundly different meanings the myth has generated in its long history, one cannot set some particular meaning (whether Freud's or anyone else's) as the standard.

These principles entail certain exclusions of material. If Freud is not the key to the Oedipus myth, then all that is "Oedipal" only under Freudian interpretation can be ruled out. The American game of base-ball and countless other things have been interpreted in terms of the Oedipus Complex. None of these things falls within the parameters of this book. Further, if Sophocles' *Oedipus the King* is only one version of the Oedipus myth among many, albeit the most important, then one will not be in the business of tracking every kind of adaptation of this tragedy. In Heinrich von Kleist's *Der zerbrochene Krug* ("The Broken Pitcher") (1808), a judge in an eighteenth-century Dutch village is put in the position of trying a case in which he himself is the guilty party. Despite his attempts to conceal the truth, the judicial inquiry he is obliged to conduct leads inevitably to the truth. Sophoclean allusions leave no doubt about the model. For example, the judge is clubfooted, his feet remind one of Oedipus' pierced ankles. But the story is completely unlike the story of Oedipus, and the same is true of other modern dramas often reckoned as descending from Sophocles: Torquato Tasso's *Torrismondo* (1574), Friedrich Schiller's *Braut von Messina* ("The Bride of Messina") (1803), and Henrik Ibsen's *Gengangere* ("Ghosts") (1881).

Even within parameters narrowed by these kinds of exclusion, there is a vast amount of material to discuss. It has been divided into five chronological periods: the earliest, pre-tragic Oedipus (Ch. 1); Oedipus in fifth-century tragedy (Ch. 2); Oedipus in Rome and the Middle Ages (Ch. 3); Oedipus in the Renaissance and Enlightenment (Ch. 4); Oedipus in the nineteenth and twentieth centuries (Ch. 5). This long history of the Oedipus myth displays, in one perspective, a certain continuity, and, in another, a discontinuity followed by a recovery. The agent of continuity is the Roman Seneca, whose *Oedipus* looked back to Greek models, had some currency in the Middle Ages, found many Renaissance imitators, and still sometimes reappears, as in Ted Hughes' adaptation (1969). But the European Middle Ages also mark a particular discontinuity in the tradition: for about a millennium, the Oedipus of Greek tragedy is practically forgotten, not to be rediscovered until the fifteenth and sixteenth centuries. Sophocles' *Oedipus the King* is thereafter destined to become the common text of the Oedipus myth, and the relative positions of Sophocles and Seneca in the tradition are reversed.

This book amounts, then, to an attempt at a "history of reception." Classical scholars use the term "reception" to refer to the reuse of ancient art and literature in new works. In the realm of myth, the term means creative work that brings the old story into the present. The Oedipus myth, more than any other Greek myth, invites this approach. Oedipus surpasses even Achilles and Odysseus in the degree to which he has permeated Western art, literature, and thought, starting with the Romans. Even if Hollywood makes films about the Trojan War heroes just named and not about Oedipus, the fact remains that Oedipus is the only Greek hero of whom it could be said that he is as much post-classical as classical. Oedipus has, in the many centuries since the Greeks, lived a longer life than the one he lived as a Greek, and, as nearly as one can tell, his old age has not yet begun.

KEY THEMES

1

OEDIPUS BEFORE TRAGEDY

Introducing Oedipus meant giving an abbreviated history of the Oedipus myth which jumped from Sophocles to Freud. This book aims to fill in the blanks in this history, starting with the pre-tragic Oedipus. Whereas the Oedipus myth is two-generational in Freud and almost two-generational in Sophocles' *Oedipus the King* (some scholars believe that the brief appearance of Oedipus' daughter at the end was added in some later production), it is four-generational in the earliest sources. This chapter first discusses these sources, and then turns from Oedipus in poetry to Oedipus as a cult-hero, one of the "mighty dead," a class of beings intermediate between gods and men, who have the power to harm or to help and who must be placated with offerings at their graves. In the sources for his cult, one has the spectacle of a multi-generational genealogy which reaches down to historical persons in the fifth century BC. Oedipus is in fact one of the few Greek heroes who has such a genealogy.

The grandfather of Oedipus, Labdacus, a shadowy figure, gives his name to the family – the Labdacids. In the archaic period of Greek literature (800–480 BC), three epic poems told their story. In one of them, the *Oedipodeia*, the events of the life of Oedipus, perhaps including the story of his father (see under "Laius" below), unfolded; in another, the *Thebaid*, the conflict between his sons; and in the *Epigoni*, the third, the exploits of the next generation. In this period, then, the Labdacid myth covers four generations in three epics. Homer, who refers to Oedipus twice in the *Iliad* and once in the *Odyssey*, knows him as a hero in the generation before the Trojan War.

The other great war of heroic times, besides the one at Troy, was the one fought by Oedipus' sons at Thebes for the succession to the throne. So said Hesiod, the great poet of didactic epic in the archaic period, who was often paired with Homer. From Hesiod, one might draw the inference that the war for the succession was the high point of Labdacid myth, and the story of Oedipus a lead-up.

Although the evidence for the myth in the archaic period is scanty, it is possible to reconstruct from this evidence a version different in remarkable ways from its embodiment in the Theban tragedies of Aeschylus, Sophocles, and Euripides. This reconstruction begins with the brief life of Oedipus which turns up in the *Odyssey* (11.271–80). Brief though it is, it provides a way of organizing the evidence from the rest of archaic poetry – fragments of Theban epic and of two lyric poets, Ibycus and Stesichorus, and also a mention of Oedipus in the *Iliad*. Odysseus tells the story of how he descended into the underworld, where he saw some of the heroines of the past and amongst them Jocasta, here called Epikastē:

> And I saw the mother of Oedipus, fair Epikastē, 271
> who committed an enormity through her mind's ignorance, 272
> marrying her own son. He, having killed [verb *exenarizō*] his father, 273
> married her. Suddenly the gods made it known amongst men. 274
> But he in lovely Thebes suffering woes [*algea*] 275
> ruled the Cadmeans [Thebans] through the destructive counsels [*boulas*] of the gods, 276
> and she went down to the house of Hades, mighty gate-fastener, 277
> having strung up a high noose from a lofty beam, 278
> gripped by her sorrow [*akhos*]. To him she left woes [*algea*] behind, 279
> very many, as many as the Erinyes of a mother bring to pass. 280

Odysseus' story of Oedipus is almost complete in three lines: Epikastē unwittingly married her son; he had killed his father; the gods suddenly made it known (272–74). Odysseus then takes six more lines to recount the aftermath: Oedipus continued to rule, suffering woes which were left to him by Epikastē, who hanged herself (275–80).

Compressed though it is, this narrative, with its repetition of the word *algea*, "woes" (275, 279), clearly signals the theme that would continue to shape it were it expanded to the length of an epic. The word which refers to the woes of Oedipus is the same one which, in the second line of the *Iliad*, refers to the "countless woes" of the Achaeans and thus to a central theme of that poem. Another comparison with the *Iliad* emerges from the word *akhos*, "sorrow," referring in the passage just quoted to the sorrow of Oedipus' mother (279). This word probably constitutes the first element in the name Achilles.[1] As Achilles is in large part the cause of the Achaeans' suffering, when he withdraws from the fighting and leaves his comrades vulnerable to the Trojans, Epikastē's sorrow, as described by Odysseus, is the beginning of Oedipus' woes. The theme of Labdacid suffering also appears in Stesichorus and Ibycus, composers of lyric verse intended, unlike epic, to be sung in choral performance. In a fragment of a lyric "Thebaid" by Stesichorus, the word *algea* turns up again. Jocasta uses it in a phrase that may refer to pains already suffered (whether by herself or by Oedipus or by both). Ibycus uses the woes (plural of *akhos*) of Oedipus as an example of the extremity of human passion.[2]

Odysseus' mention of the "woes" of Oedipus is enough to provide the thematic structure which the myth would have had in archaic poetry. Even if Odysseus does not mention a plague in Thebes (which first appears, in our sources, in Sophocles' *Oedipus the King*), comparison with the *Iliad* suggests that, thematically, a plague could already be implicit in the "woes" which he mentions. Further, Odysseus' brief summary of the Oedipus myth establishes a dynamic of transfer to be seen again and again in the history of the Oedipus myth in ancient Greek poetry. Epikastē (as the mother is here called) has, in effect, transferred her pain to Oedipus, and he, as will be clear in sources soon to be discussed, transfers his to others. The agents of Epikastē's transfer are the Erinyes, minor female deities, sometimes referred to in the plural, sometimes in the singular. They are personified curses who see to the retribution of wrongs, especially murders, committed in the family.[3] (The Erinys [sing.] was born from the blood of the severed genitals of Uranus, thus from the crime of a son against a father [Hes. *Theog.* 472].) Orestes is hounded by them in Aeschylus' *Eumenides*. At the beginning of the *Odyssey*, Telemachus fears that, if he gives in to the suitors and offers his mother in marriage to one of them, she will invoke the Erinyes against him (2.134–36). Given the dynamic of transfer, it is not surprising that its typical agents, the Erinyes, turn up in most of the ancient sources for the Oedipus myth (see below).

LAIUS

Odysseus does not name the father of Oedipus. He was Laius, who, as it happens, does not appear in the extant fragments of archaic epic. Some scholars believe that the *Oedipodeia* included a story about him known from later sources: Laius was hired by Pelops of Pisa, in northwest Greece, to train his son, Chrysippus in chariot-driving. Laius abducted and raped the boy. The source which is believed to link this story to the *Oedipodeia* is the fragment of an unidentified ancient historian or mythographer called Peisander.[4] The lengthy fragment going under his name poses a multitude of scholarly problems. For present purposes, it is enough to observe that Peisander, with mention of Oedipus' children from Euryganeia (a second wife, to be discussed below), certainly shows knowledge of the *Oedipodeia*. At the same time, he has used other (unnamed) sources, and whether the story about Laius came from one of these, and not from the *Oedipodeia*, will probably never be known. Peisander says nothing of Pelops' curse on Laius, which, with Zeus' backing, took the form of an oracle received by Laius warning that he would be killed by his own son if he were to beget one (see Aeschylus' "Theban Trilogy" in the next chapter).

RECONSTRUCTING THE STORY

Odysseus is, in the first place, telling a story, the same story or a variant of the same story told in the *Thebaid* and the *Oedipodeia*. A few fragments of these Theban epics survive, and they provide a way of filling in some of the blanks in Odysseus' synopsis. Another way is inference, which permits one to say something about how the story began.

If the marriage of Oedipus and Jocasta (as I shall call her from now on, using her regular name in fifth-century tragedy) took place in ignorance, presumably the parricide did, too. If Oedipus did not know his parents, he must have been separated from them at birth. He would then have been left to die (whether or not mutilated is unclear), only to be rescued, raised by foster parents, and then return to his native land or city. Something must have caused the exposure. The Delphic oracle, as in Sophocles, is not the obvious motivation. Greek myth and Greek epic took shape long before Delphi became the oracular center of Greece. It is mentioned explicitly only once in the *Iliad* (9.404–5) and once in the *Odyssey* (8.79–82) and would not have had any greater importance in Theban epic. It cannot be assumed to be implicit in Odysseus' summary of the myth. Perhaps a dream, Jocasta's or Laius', or a prophecy delivered by the illustrious Theban seer Teiresias (on whom see below) led to the exposure.

Between the parricide and the marriage falls Oedipus' destruction of the Sphinx, of which Odysseus says nothing. But one of the two fragments of the *Oedipodeia* places her squarely in the myth. She killed Haemon, the son of Creon, the brother of Jocasta, presumably before Oedipus came along. (Sophocles brings Haemon back to life to be the fiancé of Antigone, Oedipus' daughter.) Had Haemon failed to solve her riddle? Was she indeed a riddler? The fragment does not say. Mention of Creon suggests that he had a role to play, presumably the same one as in other sources, that of regent in the period after the death of Laius and before the accession of Oedipus.

THE SPHINX

The Sphinx, under the name Phix, appears in a genealogy of monsters in Hesiod's *Theogony*. She is a "bane to the Cadmeans," i.e., the Thebans (326). Hesiod says no more. He mentions neither her riddle nor Oedipus. The earliest vase paintings of this specifically Theban sphinx, as distinguished from the many earlier sphinxes in Greek art, which go back to Egypt and/or the Near East, show her pursuit or capture of Theban youths. Typically this monster has a lion's body, a female human head, and wings. At the time of these paintings (sixth c. BC), the Theban epics were already widespread, and so it is impossible that those who saw the vases did not think of the Oedipus myth.

The question remains of how, in their minds, Oedipus succeeded in liberating Thebes from this nuisance. When Oedipus himself appears vis-à-vis the Sphinx for the first time on a vase, in about 540 BC, he is the riddle-solver, facing her without a weapon.[5] The vast majority of vases showing Oedipus and the Sphinx – and other scenes from his life are almost non-existent – depict him thus. Should one then conclude that the riddle-solving was already in Theban epic?

It happens that one poet, Corinna, says that Oedipus actually killed the Sphinx (and also an elusive fox) by force (fr. 672 *PMG*), and in a few fifth-century vase paintings Oedipus is thrusting a spear at her.[6] Thus, like every other Greek hero who killed a monster, he is using a weapon. Should one conclude that this handful of attestations reflects an earlier tradition, still in Theban epic, which was replaced by riddle-solving? Unfortunately, this question cannot be decided. On the one hand, it is impossible to prove that the vase painters invented the motif of physical combat between Oedipus and the Sphinx; on the other, the existence of the vases, with the corroboration of the poetess (of perhaps the third c. BC), is not quite enough to allow the conclusion that this form of monster-slaying was the earlier, epic one.[7]

Despite all these doubts, the place of the Sphinx in the logic of the Oedipus myth is clear enough. She provides a motivation for the marriage of Oedipus to Jocasta. Though Oedipus killed his father, the king of Thebes, the absence of the king by itself was not enough to bring about Oedipus' marriage to the king's widow, nor, apparently, was his status as the son of the king of Corinth. The myth presupposes that he had to win the Thebans' gratitude in order to marry their queen. When he slays the monster who has been carrying off young Thebans one by one, they give him Jocasta as a reward.

THE RIDDLE OF THE RIDDLE

The famous riddle of the Sphinx is perhaps attested for the first time in an inscription on a fragmentary vase of 520–510 BC and next, clearly, in the best-known of all vase paintings of Oedipus, a cup from ca. 470 BC (fig. 3).[8] The riddle must already have been well-known, because the vase painter can reduce it to a citation of two words. The complete form is preserved in *The Learned Banquet* of Athenaeus (second c. AD), who gives as his source Asclepiades' *Tragōdoumena* ("Subjects of Tragedy") (mid-fourth c. BC):

> There walks on land a creature of two feet and four feet, which has a single voice,
> And it also has three feet; alone of the animals on earth it changes its nature,
> Of animals on the earth, in the sky, and in the sea.
> When it walks propped on the most feet,
> Then is the speed of its limbs least.[9]

Figure 3 Oedipus (here "Oedipodes") and the Sphinx. Attic red figure cup. Part of the riddle is quoted ("and three"). Vatican 16.541. Drawing by Susan Edmunds.

The answer is man, who crawls on all fours as a child, walks on two feet through most of his life, and with a cane (a third "foot") in old age. Asclepiades, who quotes the riddle as lines of epic verse, may have found it in the *Oedipodeia.* Though it is always spoken of as "the riddle of the Sphinx," it was not really her property. It was not even Greek property.[10] It has been recorded in many places – in Sumatra, the Philippine Islands, and sub-Saharan Africa.[11] This riddle has led a footloose, international existence, as it must have done in antiquity. One has to imagine that, at some point, a poet or storyteller had the clever idea of making the Sphinx pose this riddle to the Thebans on the condition answer or die. Furthermore, it was not the only riddle of which the Sphinx was capable. A fragment from an *Oedipus* by the fourth-century tragedian Theodectes gives another one: "There are two sisters, of whom one bears the other, and, having borne her, is then borne by her" (fr. 4 Snell). The answer: night and day.

As Oedipus is unparalleled amongst Greek heroes as a riddle-solver, so the Sphinx is unparalleled amongst Greek monsters as the poser of a riddle. What would have inspired someone to attach a riddle to the Sphinx? To answer the question, one has to think again of the logic of the narrative – the Sphinx as the link between parricide and incestuous marriage. The riddle motif ought somehow to reinforce the link. Indeed, it does, if one remembers one of the typical kinds of riddle in folklore, namely, the Bride-Winning-Riddle.[12] The princess poses an answer-or-die riddle to her suitors, like Turandot in the opera named after her. At some point in the history of the Oedipus myth, this kind of riddle was attached to the Sphinx. Having solved the riddle, Oedipus wins not a princess but a widowed queen for his bride.

"STRAIGHTWAY THE GODS MADE IT KNOWN"

In Odysseus' version, no time is allowed for Oedipus and his mother to produce children. Somehow the marriage is soon discovered to be incestuous and is abrogated. Presumably Oedipus then undergoes one of the several forms of purification available in Greek religious practice, and, purified, is entitled to continue as king. Pausanias, in his *Description of Greece* (second c. AD), reports that the children of Oedipus were born from a second wife, Euryganeia (9.5.10). For this fact, he refers to the *Oedipodeia*, though without quotation. He also refers to a painting of Euryganeia by Onasias (second quarter of fifth c. BC). She looks on as her sons face each other in combat. This poem and/or the tradition which it embodies are undoubtedly the source for the fifth-century genealogist, Pherecydes, who reports the same second marriage, after an interval specified as one year (the period of purification?), with the same offspring.[13]

To continue with Odysseus' synopsis, the brief incestuous marriage is a crime ("an enormity") sufficient in Jocasta's case, though unintentional, to cause her to commit suicide but insufficient in Oedipus' case to remove him from the kingship. His reign continues. If he lives on as king, presumably he is not blind. But the myth is uninterested in any further events until the death of Oedipus.

In a variant of his death attested in both Homer and Hesiod, one which fits well with his continued reign, Oedipus dies in Thebes, and his funeral rites include athletic contests. These were a way of honoring the deceased, and required a great expenditure of effort and wealth on the part of those who managed them, as Achilles did for Patroclus in the *Iliad* (23.257–897) and as others did for Achilles (*Od.* 24.85–92). In time, these funeral contests evolved into the Olympic games and similar Panhellenic festivals. The *Iliad* refers in passing to funeral games celebrated in honor of Oedipus. Euryalus, one of the Argive leaders, accepts a challenge from a Trojan to single combat (23.678–80). Homer introduces Euryalus with his genealogy.

> So he [the Trojan] spoke, and all fell silent.
> Euryalus alone rose up to face him, a godlike man,
> son of Mēkisteus, the king, son of Talaus,
> who [i.e., Mēkisteus] once came to Thebes when Oedipus had died,[14]
> for his burial. There he defeated all the Cadmeans [Thebans].

Mēkisteus belongs to the same generation as Polynices and Eteocles. So Oedipus lived two generations before the Trojan War. This chronology fits well with the genealogy of Oedipus which can be established on the basis of other sources (see fig. 1, p. xvii).

Hesiod, in his *Catalogue of Women*, told that Argeia, daughter of Adrastus, king of Argos, came to the funeral of Oedipus (fr. 192 M-W = 24 Loeb). She would later marry Polynices, after he was driven out of Thebes by his brother, and her father, Adrastus, would become one of the seven chieftains of the army which tried in vain to restore

Polynices to the throne. It was, one can assume, the war mentioned above, "over the flocks of Oedipus," referred to by Hesiod in his *Works and Days* (156–169b).

THE CURSE OF OEDIPUS ON HIS SONS

The mutual slaughter of Polynices and Eteocles in that war is the outcome of Oedipus' anger against them. Two fragments of the lost epic *Thebaid* describe outbursts on his part, each time because of the sons' mode of serving him, wine in one fragment and meat in the other. In one, he prays to Zeus that they may kill each other. In the other, he curses his sons. Though this fragment breaks off before the curse is concluded, it would undoubtedly have stipulated the same outcome for the sons as the prayer to Zeus.

> When he perceived the haunch, he threw it on the ground and spoke.
> "Alas, my sons, greatly reproaching me, sent. . . ." [A line or more is missing.]
> He prayed to Zeus and the other immortals
> that by each others' hands they go down into Hades.[15]

The scene presupposes a sacrifice and the roasting and/or the usual distribution of the parts of the sacrificial victim; further, that Oedipus was owed an honorific part.[16] The haunch, considered undesirable, is an insult to him. Whether or not the insult was intentional is unclear. The main difficulty of the fragment, however, is the circumstances under which his sons are obliged to send Oedipus a portion of the sacrifice. Is he still king? If so, this episode (and likewise the curse dramatized in the other fragment) could easily fit into the narrative which has already been reconstructed. (Oedipus' anger seems to be irrelevant to the identity of the mother of his sons. It does not matter whether she was Jocasta or Euryganeia.) Or is he living under house arrest in Thebes, as at the end of Sophocles' *Oedipus the King* and as in Euripides' *Phoenician Women*, with some remaining entitlements? If so, the sons have already begun the experiment in alternating kingship (known from later sources) which is now going to break down, thanks to the anger of Oedipus. Their deaths and a new interregnum are the climax of the sons' story, a climax which seems to displace any possibility of funeral games for Oedipus.

To turn to the fragment containing the curse, it poses, in the first place, the question of the provocation of Oedipus. Why, in the following, do the utensils inspire such a strong reaction?

> But the Zeus-born hero, golden-haired Polynices
> first set beside Oedipus the beautiful table,
> the silver one, of god-minded Cadmus. But then
> he filled a beautiful golden cup with wine.
> But when he perceived that, set beside him, were his father's
> prized gifts of honor, a great ill fell on his spirit,
> and forthwith on both his sons curses,
> terrible ones, he imprecated – it [or he] did not escape the swift Erinys' notice –
> that they might not in loving kindness their inheritance
> divide, but that for both wars and battles. . . .[17]

The answer to the question about the utensils probably lies in the phrase "his father's." Oedipus would have forbidden his sons to serve him with these utensils. Whether intentionally or not (again unclear), they disobey him. It is not the disobedience itself, however, but the concrete reminder of Laius which provokes Oedipus' reaction. As soon as Oedipus recognizes the utensils, a "great ill" falls on his spirit, and this "great ill" is the pain caused by the reminder. The curse arises immediately from this pain, and activates the Erinys (singular). The same transfer of pain, with the same prospective agent, as in the passage from the *Oedipodeia* has taken place again, this time from father to sons.

Whether or not these two fragments presuppose that Oedipus is blind is another question. The verbs of perception do not permit a definite answer.[18]

"THROUGH THE DESTRUCTIVE COUNSELS OF THE GODS"

The parallelism of curse and prayer to Zeus in the two fragments of the *Thebaid* just discussed offers a clue to the understanding of a somewhat opaque phrase in the passage from the *Odyssey*, "through the destructive counsels [*boulas*] of the gods." It is not obvious what Odysseus intends when he inserts this theological perspective into his recounting of the story of Jocasta and her son. With the *Thebaid* in mind, however, one can see immediately that he is offering a double motivation for the sufferings of Oedipus. At the human level, they are caused by Jocasta or more precisely by the transfer of her suffering to him, with the help of the Erinyes. At the divine level, the sufferings of Oedipus have some unspecified sanction, which, one assumes, would be clear if we had the whole *Oedipodeia*.

Indeed, the phrase "through the destructive counsels of the gods" is shorthand for a narrative theme, like the word *algea*. Again, comparison with the opening of the *Iliad* is illuminating, and this time it will be helpful to have the first five lines of that epic before one's eyes:

> Sing, goddess, the wrath of Achilles, son of Peleus,
> the destructive wrath, which set countless woes [*algea*] on the Achaeans,
> and sent forth many brave souls to Hades,
> souls of heroes, and left their bodies as the takings of beasts
> and every bird, and the plan [*boulē*] of Zeus was fulfilled.

The wrath of Achilles caused the woes of the Achaeans, and, says the poet in conclusion, "the plan [*boulē*, sing. of *boulas*] of Zeus was fulfilled." In the case of the *Iliad*, one knows what Zeus' plan is: to honor Achilles and his mother Thetis by making the Trojans victorious for a time, but only until the death of his friend Patroclus inspires Achilles to take up arms again. The poet even spells it out from time to time, as if to remind his audience of the higher-order causality at work in the poem. The Oedipus myth, too, it can be assumed, in its epic form or forms, would have offered a similar causal framework, within which the transfer of pain was acted out at the human level.

THE SONS OF THE SEVEN; TEIRESIAS

Polynices left a son, Thersander, who grew up in exile and then, like his father, gathered an army in order to restore himself to the throne of Thebes. The leaders of this army were the Epigoni, the sons of the Seven, and their campaign was the subject of the epic named after them. They succeeded where their fathers had failed. Two of them, Sthenelus and Diomedes, then fought at Troy (*Il.* 4. 403–10). Thersander had died at the time of the Achaeans' first attempt to reach Troy. Again, one notes that the Trojan War falls in the generation after the sons or sons/brothers, if they are the children of Jocasta (cf. on Mēkisteus p. 21).

The mythographer Apollodorus gives a detailed account of the campaign of the Epigoni (3.7.2–4). Teiresias, who would have been a major figure in the epics already discussed but happens not to appear in any of the fragments or testimonia, has a role to play in the aftermath of the battle. The seer advises the Thebans, whose army has been defeated by the Epigoni, to flee their city, and he goes with them. When they reach a spring called Tilphusa, he drinks from it and dies. Pausanias saw Teiresias' grave near this spring (9.33.1). The Epigoni, having vowed to dedicate to Apollo the fairest of the spoils from Thebes, send Manto, the daughter of Teiresias, to Delphi. A fragment of the *Epigoni* carries her story on to marriage and a new home in Colophon (fr. 3 Bernabé = 3 Davies = fr. 4 Loeb).

ENTER APOLLO

Apollo appears for the first time as an agent in the Oedipus myth in the fragment of Stesichorus (sixth c. BC) quoted above. In the best-preserved part of the fragment, a stretch of thirty-one lines, the mother of Polynices and Eteocles, addressing Teiresias, says, "May the lord Apollo, the far-worker, not bring to completion all of your prophecies" (209–10). Already, then, Teiresias has the close association with Apollo which he will have in Sophocles' *Oedipus the King*. The so-called "Apollonization" of the myth has begun. Is the mother Jocasta or Euryganeia? It is impossible to tell. If it is Jocasta, then Stesichorus' version differs markedly from the one in the *Odyssey* which this chapter has been unfolding. If it is Euryganeia, Stesichorus is consistent with the *Oedipodeia*. One recalls the painting by Onasias, in which the mother witnesses the deaths of her sons, as, one expects, the mother in Stesichorus' poem will do.

Teiresias has prophesied the mutual slaughter of the two sons (211). This prophecy does not exclude Oedipus' curse as known from the *Thebaid* – Teiresias might, in effect, be confirming its efficacy. Oedipus is mentioned, however, neither by the woman nor by Teiresias in his (not so well-preserved) speech, and it seems that Stesichorus, composing not an epic but a lyric poem, has refocused the myth on the relation of mother and sons. In Euripides' *Phoenician Women*, Jocasta commits suicide after she witnesses their end (1455–59), and perhaps Stesichorus' poem ended in the same way.

THE CULTS OF OEDIPUS AND OF OEDIPUS AND LAIUS

Oedipus was a hero in three senses of the word. First, he belonged to the race of the heroes, as in Hesiod's chronology of the five races of man in his *Works and Days*. The passage has already been referred to in connection with the war "over the flocks of Oedipus." The heroes were the fourth race, which, Hesiod says, was partly destroyed in the wars at Thebes and Troy. Second, Oedipus was also a hero in the sense that he was the protagonist of a lost epic poem, the *Oedipodeia*. Finally, he was a hero of cult, worshipped in several places in Greece. The sons of Oedipus also had a cult, in Thebes. Oedipus and his father were joined in a cult in Sparta.

These cults provide an introduction to Sophocles' *Oedipus at Colonus*, to be introduced below and further discussed in the next chapter. This tragedy culminates in the establishment of a peculiar hero cult of Oedipus in Athens. Even without this tragedy, however, the cults of Oedipus at Thebes and Sparta would be important for what they show about the myth of Oedipus. The phenomenon of parallel myths and cults has turned up in many parts of the world, and anthropologists have often been able to observe that the two are functionally similar.[19] The same will be true of the myth and cults of

Oedipus. The latter embody, in a particular institution of Greek religion, exactly the same issue which emerges again and again in the myth: the trans-generational curse of suffering. The cults show how the sins of the father are visited not only on the sons but also on many succeeding generations.

The cults of Oedipus and of Oedipus and his father associate him with two deities. One, not surprisingly, is the Erinys (sometimes imagined as singular, sometimes as plural, i.e., Erinyes). The other is Demeter. At first, the two deities, and thus the two cults, seem unrelated. In fact, it will turn out that, just as Oedipus is associated with each of these deities, they are independently associated with each other, so that the three together constitute a notional trinity.

A story concerning a cult of Oedipus in a precinct of Demeter:

> When Oedipus died and his friends intended to bury him in Thebes, the Thebans prevented them because of the earlier misfortunes, on the grounds that it was impious. His friends, having taken him to a certain place in Boeotia [the region of Greece in which Thebes is located] called Ceos, buried him. When certain misfortunes befell those living in the village, thinking that the cause was the grave of Oedipus, they ordered Oedipus' friends to remove him from the place. Bewildered by these events, the friends took him up and conveyed him to Eteonos. Wanting to conduct the burial secretly, they bury him at night in a shrine of Demeter, not recognizing the spot. When it became known, the inhabitants of Eteonos asked the god [Apollo] what they should do. The god replied that they should not disturb the "suppliant" [on this account he is buried there] of the goddess and that the shrine be called Oedipodeion.[20]

Though Oedipus dies in Thebes, as in the myth reconstructed above, he is far from eligible for funeral games. He cannot even be buried in his native city. Certain unidentified friends take him to another place, Ceos, a town southeast of Thebes, where his grave causes unspecified misfortunes. Then they take his remains to Eteonos, a town near Mt. Cithaeron, where he is finally settled, thanks to Apollo, in a precinct sacred to Demeter. Here is more evidence for the "Apollonization" of the myth, which was noticed for the first time in Stesichorus (sixth c. BC). A hero's sharing a precinct with a god or goddess is in itself unremarkable. The practice is well attested for ancient Greece. It can be compared with the worship of saints in the chapels in Catholic churches. Oedipus as a "supplicant" of the goddess requires more explanation. In Sophocles' *Oedipus at Colonus*, the old Oedipus, arriving at a sacred grove in a town outside Athens, realizes that here is his destined resting place (84–110), and yet he has to present himself as a suppliant to the townsfolk in order to be allowed to stay (275–91, 487). Oedipus' suppliancy (in Apollo's figure of speech) at Eteonos is of the same order: the unwitting burial of Oedipus in the precinct of Demeter amounts to a petition on his part that he be allowed to remain, having been displaced from his native Thebes and then from Ceos.

The burial of Oedipus is associated with Demeter in two other sources. One is the tragedy of Sophocles just mentioned. In the space offstage, visible from the space in which the drama unfolds, "the hill of Demeter" can be seen (1600). Androtion, one of the so-called "Atthidographers," local historians of Attica, writing in the fourth century BC, says explicitly that Oedipus was a suppliant of Demeter at Colonus: "Oedipus, banished from Thebes by Creon, came to Attica and dwelt in the so-called Hill of the Horseman [Colonus]. And he was a suppliant in the shrine of the goddesses Demeter and Poliouchos [lit. "City-holding"] Athena. . . ."[21] Androtion thus provides a clear parallelism to the burial at Eteonos.

The association of Oedipus with the Erinyes in cult takes two forms. One is juxtaposition. In *Oedipus at Colonus*, Oedipus dies and is buried in a grove sacred to the Erinyes (here called by their friendlier names "Eumenides," "Kindly Ones" [42, 487] and "Semnai," "Awful Ones" or "Revered Ones" [90, 100, 458]). (The word "Erinys" is reserved in this tragedy for Polynices, who uses it twice, once in the singular and once in the plural, of his father's anger against him: 1299, 1434.) A rival cult in Athens placed the grave of Oedipus on the hill called Areopagus. Pausanias reports on a monument of Oedipus within a sanctuary of the Erinyes ("whom the Athenians call the Semnai, but Hesiod calls the Erinyes") on Areopagus (1.18.6–7). The founders of the cult had brought Oedipus' bones, like a saint's relics, from Thebes. Pausanias is well aware of the contradiction between this story of the origin of the Areopagus cult and the story dramatized by Sophocles, in which Oedipus arrives at a suburb of Athens under his own locomotion and then dies there. Citing Homer (the passage on the funeral games for

Oedipus) against Sophocles, Pausanias opts for burial in Thebes and thus implies the spuriousness of the cult at Colonus.

The other form of association with the Erinyes is closer. Oedipus has his own Erinys, which he activated with his curse on his sons. Laius, too, has his Erinys, activated by Oedipus' murder of him. In a fragment of a tragedy by Aeschylus, perhaps his *Oedipus* (but assigned to the category of "uncertain" by the most recent editor Radt [fr. 387a]), Oedipus killed Laius at Potniai, "Queens," a town near Thebes named after Demeter and her daughter, Korē (Paus. 9.8.1). The Erinyes were also worshipped there (Eur. *Or.* 317–18; cf. *Phoen.* 1124–25). Oedipus thus killed his father directly under the eyes of the deities who would be quickest to torment the perpetrator of such a crime, as the poet Pindar observes in a passage to be quoted below.

The Erinyes could have cults, as at Colonus and on the Areopagus and in many other places, and the Erinyes of particular persons, like Oedipus and Laius, could also have cults. The fifth-century BC historian Herodotus tells at considerable length of the founding of a cult in Sparta to the Erinyes of these two (4.147–50; cf. Paus. 9.5.14–15). The story entails their distant descendants and is best grasped with the aid of the family tree (cf. fig. 1). Polynices left a son. The grandson of this son migrated to Sparta. In the fourth (or perhaps later) generation thereafter, because of the stillbirths of their children, the descendants of this family erect a temple in honor of the Erinyes of Laius and Oedipus. They believe that they are under a curse going all the way back to these remote forebears.

Another descendant of this family was Theron, the tyrant of the Sicilian city Acragas (modern Agrigento) (again see fig. 1). Pindar composed an ode to celebrate his victory in the chariot race at the Olympic games of 476 BC. He summarizes the extended Oedipus myth to illustrate a favorite theme, the alternations of human happiness. Destiny, Pindar says,

> with wealth that springs from the gods
> brings also some pain, itself to turn around another time,
> ever since the son foretold by fate killed Laius,
> encountering him, and what had been prophesied at Delphi
> long ago was fulfilled.

> Seeing, the sharp Erinys
> killed his warlike offspring [i.e., Polynices and Eteocles] in mutual slaughter.
> There was left Thersander to Polynices after he had been brought down, in later contests
> and in war's battles acquiring honor. . . . (*Olympian* 2.35–45)

After the positive example of Thersander, Pindar jumps forward to the present and to the victorious Theron. Pindar's version of the parricide is the point which concerns the present discussion. The poet creates a direct link between the parricide, which activates the Erinys of Laius, and the deaths of Oedipus' sons.

The cults of Oedipus thus show an association with both Demeter and the Erinyes. These deities are already themselves associated independently of Oedipus. In *Oedipus at Colonus*, their sanctuaries are geographically contiguous. At Potniai, they form a group. Demeter could even take the form of the Erinys, as she did when she mated with Poseidon (Apollodorus 3.6.8). So Oedipus, Demeter, and the Erinyes constitute a trinity. The unexpected element in this trinity is Demeter, whose brief mention in Sophocles' tragedy would never, by itself, have suggested that she was integral to the mythical and/or cultic conception of Oedipus. Undoubtedly it is her chthonic aspect and her closeness to the Erinyes which connected her with him.

The cults and myth of Oedipus present a remarkable consistency. The Erinyes, who in the myth respond to the wrongful death of a parent (Jocasta, Laius) and torment the son (Oedipus) or to the curse of a parent (Oedipus) and torment the sons (Polynices, Eteocles), torment future generations in real life (Autesion, the Aegids) and have to be propitiated in cult. The distinction between myth and real life is not, however, one which ancient Greeks would readily have made. If a child or grandchild of Theron happened to be in Athens and saw the performance of Sophocles' *Oedipus the King*, he or she would have believed that the protagonist of the tragedy was a remote ancestor, a historical person, not a fictional or, as we would say, a mythical one.

OVERVIEW

Suffering, which seems to supervene unexpectedly upon a hitherto prosperous Oedipus in Sophocles' tragedy, is a primitive, pervasive trait in the myth. The pre-tragic myth of Oedipus is not only about Oedipus but concerns the whole story of the Labdacids from the time of Laius. Though epic divided the story of the first three generations into two parts, with Laius (apparently) and Oedipus in the *Oedipodeia* and the sons of Oedipus in the *Thebaid*, the story is continuous. The suffering which is stamped on the Labdacids from the time of Laius and the curse of Pelops continues down through the ages. The stories attached to the cults allow one to follow its course down into historical times. Pindar took the most optimistic view: not every generation has to suffer, some generations will prosper. Nevertheless, the dynamic of transfer is hereditary. On a pessimistic view, equally plausible, the Erinyes of the Labdacids are like a gene which in happy times is recessive. The offspring of Theron have to worry that it may produce new phenotypes, new forms of suffering like the stillbirths of the Aegids.

2

OEDIPUS ON STAGE: FIFTH-CENTURY TRAGEDY

The medium of tragedy, coming into existence in Athens at the end of the sixth century, puts the Oedipus myth in a new trajectory, the one which, with the rediscovery of Greek tragedy in the Renaissance, carries it up to the present. The new dramatic form, highly compressed in comparison with epic, focuses on the climactic events of a single day. The audience already knows the stories, and narrative comes in only when a character has to explain something that happened earlier, before today's events.

Author	Kind of work	Title(s) fr.: work survives only in fragments ti: work known by title only	Century (BC unless otherwise noted)
Aeschylus	tragedy	*Eumenides*, fr. *Laius*, fr. *Oedipus*, *Seven Against Thebes*, fr. *Sphinx*	5th
Androtion	local history of Attica	fr. *Atthis*	4th
Anonymous	epic	fr. *Epigoni*	6th
Anonymous	epic	fr. *Oedipodeia*	6th
Anonymous	epic	fr. *Thebaid*	6th
Antimachus of Colophon	epic, elegy	fr. *Thebaid*, fr. *Lydē*	5th

Apollodorus	mythography	*Library*	2nd AD
Aristophanes	comedy	*Acharnians*	5th
Aristotle	philosophy	*Poetics*	4th
Asclepiades	mythography	fr. *Tragōdoumena*	4th
Astydamas	tragedy	ti. *Antigone*	4th
Athenaeus	symposium	*The Learned Banquet*	2nd–3rd AD
Corinna	lyric	unknown	uncertain
Diogenes the Cynic	tragedy	ti. *Oedipus*	4th
Euripides	tragedy	fr. *Antigone,* fr. *Chrysippus, Orestes,* fr. *Oedipus, Phoenician Women, Suppliants*	5th
Herodotus	history	*Histories*	5th
Hesiod	didactic epic, genealogy	*Works and Days, Theogony,* fr. *Catalogue of Women*	8th
Homer	epic	*Iliad, Odyssey*	8th
Ibycus	lyric	untitled	6th
Ion of Chios	dithyrambic	*Dithyrambs*	5th
Lysimachus	history	*Thebaica*	3rd–2nd
Meletus	tragedy	ti. *Oedipodeia*	4th
Mimnermus	lyric poetry	untitled	7th
Nicarchus	epigram	untitled	1st
Pausanias	geographical description	*Description of Greece*	2nd AD
Peisander	history or mythography	untitled	unknown
Pherecydes	genealogy	no surviving titles	5th
Philip	epigram	untitled	1st–1st AD
Pindar	choral lyric	*Olympians*	5th
Sophocles	tragedy	*Oedipus the King, Antigone, Oedipus at Colonus,* fr. *Epigoni*	5th
Stesichorus	choral lyric	untitled	6th
Theodectes	tragedy	fr. *Oedipus*	4th
Xenocles	tragedy	ti. *Oedipus*	5th

Figure 4 Greek sources for the Oedipus myth.

Of the two main genres of poetry surveyed in the preceding chapter, epic and lyric, one ceases to have importance for Oedipus. Lyric poetry does not take him as a subject again after Pindar. Though the archaic epics were still current in the fifth century, their importance for Oedipus becomes a matter of their reuse by the tragedians. Aeschylus famously said that his plays were only scraps from Homer's banquet. If "Homer" stands for all of archaic epic including the Theban branch, Aeschylus' remark applies quite well to his Oedipus trilogy, to be discussed below. Antimachus of Colophon composed a new *Thebaid*. About seventy lines survive, none of them, unfortunately, revealing anything about his version of the Oedipus myth. His narrative elegy (a genre, like lyric, on the way out) called *Lydē*, for his deceased wife or mistress, told of several mythical heroes, including Oedipus. A two-line fragment, of great interest for a motif concerning the youth of Oedipus, is discussed below in connection with Euripides' *Phoenician Women*.

Of several fifth-century tragedies in which Oedipus was the pro-tagonist, only Sophocles' *Oedipus the King* and *Oedipus at Colonus* survive entire. At least four other tragedians composed an Oedipus tragedy.[1] Little but the titles survives. Of Sophocles' two Oedipus tragedies, the former is by far the better known, and now amounts to "the Oedipus myth" for all except a few classicists. It would still, no doubt, have the same prestige which it has had since the Renaissance, even if the other Oedipus tragedies survived. But "the Oedipus myth" would not look exactly the same as it does now. So much can be inferred from fragments of and testimonia about the lost tragedies and above all from the three extant tragedies concerning the children of Oedipus. These sources make it possible to get a sense of the pecu-liarity of Sophocles' *Oedipus the King*, the one who was to become canonical.

AESCHYLUS' THEBAN TRILOGY

Aeschylus produced his trilogy *Laius*, *Oedipus*, and *Seven Against Thebes* in 467 BC. Only the third of these tragedies survives. The satyr play, the shorter, comic piece following a trilogy, was in this case

Sphinx. The titles alone of the three tragedies show that Aeschylus, like the epic poets, still conceived of the myth as multi-generational. His theme was also traditional, the curse on the family, which is referred to about twenty times in the course of *Seven*. With Aeschylus, however, the Delphic oracle is now squarely in the picture. The chorus of *Seven*, consisting of Theban women, sings of "new pains of the family mixed with the old." They continue: "For I tell of an ancient transgression that brought swift recompense – and that it remains until the third generation – when Laius, though Apollo thrice at Pytho [Delphi], navel of the earth, said that dying without offspring, he could save his city, overcome by fond foolishness begot destiny for himself, the parricide Oedipus" (740–52). The "transgression" might be Laius' disregard of the prophecy, or it might be a deed which could motivate the prophecy in the first place.

Such a deed is attested in an oracle quoted in the prefatory material found in many manuscripts of Euripides' *Phoenician Women*:

> Laius, son of Labdacus, you ask for the blessed offspring of children.
>
> You will beget a dear son, but this will be your doom,
>
> to quit life at the hands of your son. For thus has assented
>
> Zeus, son of Cronus, obeying the hateful curses of Pelops,
>
> whose son you abducted; and he imprecated all these things upon you.

Why did Pelops curse Laius? The story of Laius' rape of Pelops' son, Chrysippus, was told in the preceding chapter. The boy committed suicide out of shame. Pelops then cursed Laius, as in the oracle just quoted. The pederasty of Laius in itself would not have constituted an offense; it was his use of force which shamed the boy and brought down the curse of Pelops.[2]

Jocasta recalls the curse at the beginning of Euripides' tragedy (17–20). The oracle received by Laius is often referred to, as by Jocasta in Sophocles' *Oedipus the King* (711–14), though Sophocles says nothing about the rape. In the form of the oracle quoted here, Zeus backs up the curse, and curse and divine sanction are thus combined, just as with Oedipus' curse on his sons and its presumptive backing by Zeus (cf. the two fragments of the *Thebaid* discussed in the preceding chapter).

Aeschylus' *Laius*, which included at least a reference to the exposure of the infant Oedipus (fr. 12 Radt), would have ended with the death of Laius at his son's hands in fulfillment of Pelops' curse as sanctioned by Zeus, whose will was revealed to Laius by Apollo.[3] The events of *Oedipus*, the next play, can be inferred from another place in *Seven*:

> What man did they so honor,
> the gods of the city who share an altar [on the acropolis]
> and the much-attended assembly of men,
> as they then honored Oedipus,
> who rid the land
> of the man-snatching ruin [the Sphinx]?
>
> Though he had been of right mind,
> [now] miserable with the woe [*algos*]
> of a wretched marriage,
> with raging heart
> he brought to pass two ills;
> with father-slaying hand
> he deprived himself of eyes dearer than children.[4]

The marriage was incestuous, as other passages make even clearer (e.g., 928–29). This passage provides the earliest evidence for the self-blinding of Oedipus, which is the first of the two ills. It presupposes Oedipus' discovery of his crimes. The second ill will be the curse on the sons, which the chorus goes on to describe.

> And upon his sons he sent
> wretched curses, angry because of their sustenance [of him], alas,
> curses of bitter tongue,
> and that they with iron-wielding hand
> at some time divide
> his possessions.

The chorus concludes: "I fear lest now the swift-running Erinys bring it to pass" (785–91). If the chorus is referring to a curse which was dramatized in *Oedipus*, then the reason for the curse, the sons' failure to provide adequate support, must also have been dramatized, and the discovery and the self-blinding must have occurred rather early on. The curse would then have been climactic, appropriately preparing for the next play, *Seven*.

In this play, Oedipus is apparently dead (cf. 975–77) and buried in Thebes (cf. 1004). His curse and Erinys are omnipresent. The ultimate responsibility of Laius is not, however, forgotten. The messenger who reports the mutual slaughter of Eteocles and Polynices says that "Apollo took the seventh gate" of the city, "fulfilling for the offspring of Oedipus the ancient folly of Laius" (800–802). Mention of Apollo here evokes the oracle Laius disregarded, which expressed the divine sanction for Pelops' curse on Laius, as in the text of the oracle quoted above.

Aeschylus' trilogy thus powerfully affirms the archaic epic vision of the curse on the family, which brings suffering and death to one generation after another. (The artistic and thematic originality of Aeschylus in this trilogy is another matter, which lies outside the present discussion.) Yet Aeschylus seems to want to end the story with the deaths of Eteocles and Polynices. Only from the subtle interpretation of a single passage in *Seven* can it be inferred that the Epigoni, the sons of the Seven (and thus the continuation of the family as in Pindar), are still to come. Some have taken lines 740–52 (quoted above) to imply that, because the city of Thebes must be destroyed and it has not happened at the end of *Seven*, the Epigoni must be in the offing. Against this one passage, however, can be set several indications that the line of the Labdacids has come to an end. In this way, Aeschylus makes the myth fit his trilogy.

EURIPIDES

Aeschylus' trilogy was the first and last dramatization of the three-generational Labdacid myth.[5] Sophocles and Euripides composed tragedies on the separate parts of the myths, as did a certain Xenocles, who presented an *Oedipus* in 415 BC. Euripides' *Chrysippus*, of which a few fragments remain, probably dramatized the story of Pelops' curse on Laius. His *Oedipus*, also fragmentary, would have covered the same ground as the Oedipus tragedies of Aeschylus and of Sophocles. One of the fragments, to be discussed below, gives a version of the blinding of Oedipus which diverges strikingly from the *self*-blinding made canonical by Sophocles. Euripides' *Antigone*, as prefatory material in manuscripts of Sophocles' *Antigone* shows, has the heroine marry Haemon and bear a son, Maion (cf. Hyginus *Fabulae* 72). In Sophocles, both die before their marriage can take place. *Phoenician Women*, produced after 412 BC, is complete, though some or all of the final scene may be spurious. His *Suppliants* (425–422 BC) concerns the attempt of the Argive women, the wives and mothers of the Seven, to recover the corpses of their slain husbands and sons for burial, and the intercession on their behalf of the Athenian king, Theseus.

Phoenician Women

In this single tragedy, which corresponds in mythical time to Aeschylus' *Seven*, Euripides' conception of the Oedipus myth is even broader than that of Aeschylus' whole Theban trilogy. The chorus of Phoenician women after which the tragedy is named give it this breadth. As natives of Tyre in Phoenicia, they are distant kinswomen of the Thebans, because Cadmus, the founder of Thebes, was the son of Agenor, the king of the Phoenicians. The Phoenician women speak of the Thebans as Cadmeans and of the Cadmeans as Agenorids, descendants of Agenor, and they name Io, the great-grandmother of Agenor, as both their own and the Thebans' ultimate ancestress. In their vast perspective, the Thebans now about to fight outside the walls of Thebes are the "race of the Sown Men" (795), the men who sprang from the dragon's teeth sown by Cadmus.

The Phoenician women are not, however, themselves mythological figures like the main characters of the tragedy but simply fill a dramatic role. They happen to be in Thebes because they are en route to Delphi, where they will be servants of Apollo, a living offering to the god sent by their native city of Tyre. It is a coincidence that they are in Thebes at the time of Polynices' attack on the city. In this role, then, they personify the link between Theban myth and the oracle of Apollo. But nothing in the myth is beyond them, and they are also well aware of the curse and the Erinys. Early on, they say: "About the city a thick cloud of shields blazes, which Ares will soon know that he brings to the sons of Oedipus as the Erinyes' misery" (250–55). They and others often refer to the curse of Oedipus. In a part of the play which some commentators consider a later interpolation, Oedipus himself says that he inherited the curse from Laius (Pelops' on Laius? Laius' on Oedipus?) and passed it on to his sons (1611–12). The notion of a transgenerational curse was, as we have seen, already well-established in the myth.

In this tragedy, Euripides presents a version of the myth which, in large features, differs from any other. Both Jocasta and Oedipus are alive at the time of the campaign of the Seven. Jocasta as intermediary between her sons has something like the role of the mother in Stesichorus' "Thebaid," whose precise identity cannot, however, be determined. She also has something like the role of Euryganeia in the painting by Onasias (second quarter of fifth c. BC) mentioned in the last chapter, who looks on as her sons face each other in combat. Euripides perhaps conflated the non-incestuous Euryganeia with the incestuous Jocasta, who in the relevant tragedies of Aeschylus and Sophocles is already dead at the time of the campaign of the Seven. In Euripides' tragedy, his Jocasta commits suicide over the bodies of her sons. Oedipus lives on. At the end, Antigone summons him from within the palace, where he has been living under a kind of house arrest (63–65), dishonored by his sons, whom he curses (66–68, 874–77), and attended by Jocasta. Antigone refuses marriage with Haemon, Creon's son, and goes off into exile with her father. She complains about Creon's refusal of burial to Polynices but does not stay to disobey Creon and perform the burial, as she does in Sophocles' *Antigone*. In lines often considered spurious, Oedipus names Colonus as their destination (1703–7).

Euripides' largest departure from the mythical tradition has been seen not in the major characters but in Menoeceus, son of Creon, who commits suicide as a sacrifice to Ares, in order to win the god's favor for the Thebans. It is worth pausing on Menoeceus because an important issue is involved, which is the freedom of poets to create new versions of myths. Scholars sometimes speak of this Menoeceus as Euripides' "creation." It is useful to distinguish, however, between a purely imaginary, free creation and creation out of, and thus constrained by, pre-existing material. In the case of a myth, this second kind of creation would be what I have been calling variation. In the mythical tradition, Creon had three sons. It has been argued that the three are all variants of the same motif, the son who sacrifices himself.[6] Even where some scholars have seen a clear case of free creation, it seems more prudent, then, to keep open the possibility of variation within a given tradition.

To return to elements of the story of Oedipus himself, in the prologue of *Phoenician Women* Jocasta recounts the story in considerable detail. Her, or Euripides', version of the parricide, though apparently diverging from Sophocles' only in a trivial way, will prove to have important implications for Sophocles' handling of this motif. She says: "Son kills father and, taking the chariot, gives it to Polybus, who raised him" (44–45). Again, one might have suspected free elaboration on Euripides' part if the same form of the motif were not attested in Antimachus. In a two-line fragment of his *Lydē*, he has Oedipus say, "Polybus, I shall give you these horses, which I have driven off from an enemy, as recompense for my rearing" (fr. 70 W²).[7] Looking back to the summary of Oedipus' life in the *Odyssey*, one sees that the verb which refers to Oedipus' killing of Laius might be more specific than it seemed at first (*exenarizō*, p. 14). It means literally "to strip a foe slain in battle." When Homeric heroes do so, they often also try to drive off the foe's horses. Odysseus' summary might, then, presuppose the form of the motif made explicit in Euripides and in Antimachus.

Jocasta has already explained that Oedipus knew that Polybus was not his father, "either having figured it out on his own or having learned from someone else" (33). Oedipus therefore has no qualms about returning to Corinth with the spoils from his murder of Laius. Further, Jocasta makes it clear that the parricide took place before Oedipus reached Delphi, where he was going to inquire about his natural parents. In fact, she is silent about the oracle which hangs over him in Sophocles' tragedy. The implications of Euripides' version of the myth for the understanding of Sophocles' will be explored below.

Euripides' *Oedipus*

A tragedian could use different versions of the myth in different tragedies, when they were not parts of a necessarily self-consistent trilogy. (Sophocles, too, will illustrate this point.) For this reason, *Phoenician Women* cannot be taken to show anything about Euripides' fragmentary *Oedipus*. The plot of this tragedy cannot be reconstructed, though some fragments show that it presupposes a different version of the myth. In *Phoenician Women*, Oedipus blinded himself, whereas in *Oedipus* a servant of Laius says:

> having pinned the son of Polybus to the ground
> we hold open his eyes and destroy the pupils (fr. 541 Kannicht = 84 Austin)

If Oedipus can be referred to as "the son of Polybus," then he is blinded before he has discovered that he is the son of Laius and married to his own mother. The blinding is punishment for the murder of Laius and carried out by his former retainers, still loyal, who belong to the palace staff inherited by the new king, Oedipus. At what point would this event have occurred? An answer is suggested by an Etruscan urn (second c. BC) with a relief which apparently depicts the scene. Soldiers are blinding Oedipus. There are two young boys, presumably his sons, and a woman, presumably Jocasta.[8] Oedipus has, then, been king for some time when he is discovered, or discovers himself, to be the murderer of Laius – long enough for him to have young children. He will be already blind when, in the course of the tragedy, he makes the further discovery that the murder was a parricide.

Euripides might again be suspected of creating a new variant of a motif, this time the blindness of Oedipus. But the same source, a scholiast or ancient commentator on *Phoenician Women*, who preserved the fragment just quoted, also says that the blindness was the result of Oedipus' curse on the murderer. Another scholium or comment on this tragedy reports that Polybus blinded Oedipus in order to avert the prophecy he had received. In short, the motif of blindness seems not to have been firmly attached to any one agent or to any one point in the chronology of the myth. In the Odyssean version of the myth quoted in the preceding chapter, blindness was not mentioned; and there were other indications of an archaic version of the myth in which Oedipus remained sighted until the end of his life.

The question therefore arises of why the blinding of Oedipus became part of the myth in the first place, no matter how or when Oedipus was blinded. One can give an answer in terms of symbolism. It happens that eyes can symbolize genitals in Greek myth and thus, in the case of sexual transgression, can replace the offending part as the object of punishment. In the *Iliad*, the hero Phoenix says that he was rendered sterile by the Erinyes, whom his father invoked after Phoenix slept with his father's concubine (9.453–56). In the more common version of the myth, Phoenix was not sterilized but blinded (Aristophanes *Acharnians* 421; Apollodorus 3.13.8). Blinding has the same function in the myths of the hunter Orion and of Phineus. The former raped the daughter of Oinopion, and, in revenge, Oinopion blinded him. Phineus, wrongly believing that his sons had slept with their stepmother, blinded them (Apollodorus 3.15.3; cf. Soph. *Ant.* 971–73, where the stepmother blinds them, though the reason is not stated).[9] Given this particular symbolic value of the motif, its appropriateness to the Oedipus myth is obvious. It adds what the Italian scholar Giulio Guidorizzi calls a "surplus of symbolic significance."[10] In this larger comparative context, self-blinding looks like a particular variant of the generic motif of blinding as punishment for sexual crime.

A fragment accepted in the most recent editions as belonging to Euripides' *Oedipus* may attest another striking variant of the myth. Jocasta, in a speech on the duties of wife to husband, is apparently saying that she will follow Oedipus into exile:

> It is pleasing . . . if her husband has some setback, for a wife to put on a sad face with him and to join in sharing his pains and pleasures. You and I – now you are guilty of sin, I will endure your guilt and help to bear your troubles; and nothing will be (too) harsh for me.[11]

If this speech follows the discovery of incest and parricide (Oedipus having been detected as murderer of Laius before his relation to him was known), then Oedipus must presumably leave Thebes, as in other fifth-century versions of the myth, and Jocasta is saying that she will accompany him. She neither commits suicide, then, as in Homer and in Sophocles, nor stays on in Thebes until the deaths of Eteocles and Polynices, as in *Phoenician Women*, but plays the role in which we will see Antigone in Sophocles' *Oedipus at Colonus*.

SOPHOCLES AND THE OEDIPUS MYTH

Sophocles' three Theban tragedies are often referred to as a trilogy. The important point is not simply that they were not a trilogy in the ancient sense but that each has a particular autonomy with relation to the myth. Presumably the same is true of his scantily attested *Epigoni*.[12] *Oedipus the King*, with its intense focus on the central character's developing awareness of, and final discovery of, his identity and his crimes, scales the myth down to a short version. Now the myth ends with Oedipus' self-blinding. The audience does not know exactly what will happen thereafter, and, as far as the tragedy is concerned, it does not matter. Sophocles composed another tragedy, *Oedipus at Colonus*, about the end of Oedipus' life. The two Oedipus tragedies can be, but do not have to be, taken together. Sophocles' dramatization of the hero's death again scales the myth down to a short, independent unit of action, with thematic issues for the most part distinct from those of his other Oedipus tragedy. The same can be said of Sophocles' handling of the strife between the sons of Oedipus in *Antigone*. The tragedian approaches the subject, long since famous in Theban epic and already dramatized by Aeschylus, obliquely. He concentrates on the burial of one of the sons, Polynices, which his sister, Antigone, after whom the tragedy in question is named, takes it upon herself to perform. In this way, Sophocles shifts the focus of the myth to the struggles of a single character, Antigone, against the regent, Creon. Sophocles' foregrounding of this heretofore marginal character might be compared with Tom Stoppard's *Rosenkrantz and Guildenstern Are Dead*, in which two minor characters from Shakespeare's *Hamlet* become the protagonists of a new play. But because of Sophocles' tragedy, Antigone became, amongst the figures of Greek myth, one of the few to rival Oedipus in their grip on the imagination of the nineteenth and twentieth centuries. From a review of the pre-Sophoclean evidence for the Oedipus myth, the fragments of Theban epic and of archaic lyric, one would hardly know that she existed. Such is the power of Sophocles over the history of the Oedipus myth.

Sophocles' Oedipus the King

Chapters Four and Five of this book will discuss the profound impact of this tragedy, which comes to stand for "the Oedipus myth," on the modern imagination. A chapter not provided for in the plan of this book might have discussed scholarly interpretation of this tragedy as a tragedy and the never-ending struggle to determine its meaning. Charles Segal provides an overview of these matters in *Oedipus Tyrannus: Tragic Heroism and the Limits of Knowledge*.[13] The concern of the present chapter is the relation of this tragedy to the Oedipus myth in its own time and the peculiarities of Sophocles' treatment of some of the motifs.

A plague appears for the first time in the Oedipus myth at the opening of this tragedy. Because a plague fell on Athens in 429, returning in 427–426 BC, scholars have often argued that the tragic plague is modeled on the historical one, and in this way they have tried to establish a date after which the tragedy had to be composed. A poetic model certainly exists in the plague in the first Book of the *Iliad*, discussed in the preceding chapter, and the word *algos*, "woe," thematic both in the *Iliad* and inferably in the *Odyssey* summary of the Oedipus myth, returns in Sophocles at the point at which Oedipus says that he bears all the "suffering" which each of the Thebans feels individually (62–64). Oedipus will prove to be the cause of the plague, as Agamemnon, the leader of the Achaeans, is the cause of the plague in the *Iliad*. The god who sent the plague on the Achaeans was Apollo; in *Oedipus the King*, however, neither who sent the plague nor why it has come at this particular time is clear.

Sophocles abstracts from the three-generational version of the myth and therefore excludes the curse on the family. He never mentions the Erinyes, who are implied only once, when Teiresias tells Oedipus that the "terrible-footed curse" of his parents will drive him from this land (417–18). The adjective reminds of other -*pous* ("foot") compounds which describe the Erinyes. For that matter, Oedipus' own name is a *-pous* compound, which may indicate a particular affinity with the dread goddesses.[14] Sophocles continues to see Oedipus as the source of a curse, but now it is what might be called an administrative or legalistic curse. Receiving the oracle from Delphi which says that the plague can be ended only if the murderer of Laius is removed from the city, Oedipus issues an edict against this unknown person. The chorus refers to it as a curse (295), and, when Oedipus first suspects that he may be the one who killed Laius, he uses the same term to refer to his edict (744, cf. 820).

The plague is the occasion for Oedipus' consultation of the Delphic oracle, and the oracular response prompts his summoning of Teiresias, who is a mythical prototype of the seer, the specialist in predicting the future from signs, a person well-known in the Greek cities of Sophocles' day.[15] Teiresias is a fixture in the myth concerning Oedipus and his sons and daughters.[16] It is only a matter of chance that he is not mentioned in any archaic source for Labdacid myth except in Stesichorus, where he is "the god-like seer" (fr. 222b.227 Davies), just as in Sophocles, who uses the same phrase (298). While his entrance in *Oedipus the King* has a specifically dramatic motivation (282–89), ultimately his presence in this tragedy is not only motivated by but also probably even required by tradition.

Because the Oedipus myth pre-dates the importance of the Delphic oracle, someone other than Apollo must originally have made the prediction that prompted the exposure of the infant Oedipus, and that person might have been Teiresias. He would have belonged to the beginning of the story. In Sophocles' tragedy, he appears at the beginning, but not because he is expected to predict the future. Rather, Oedipus consults him on the identity of a person who has committed a crime in the past. Teiresias reluctantly complies; Oedipus denies Teiresias' incrimination of him; and then the seer falls back into his accustomed role of predicting the future. "This day will beget you and destroy you" (442). Further, Oedipus will be blind and he will go into exile and thus presumably meet his death outside of Thebes (417–21, 454–56). In this way, Teiresias defines the version of the myth that this tragedy presupposes, a version different from the one in which Oedipus dies and is buried in Thebes. After his exit at the end of this scene, Teiresias is never seen again, and he is never mentioned again after Oedipus questions Creon about him in the next scene. For all dramatic intents and purposes, he ceases to exist.

Oedipus' search for the murderer of Laius, causing him to summon Teiresias, whose words he cannot believe, leads him to suspect that the seer and Creon are plotting against him: Creon, hoping to replace Oedipus as king, sent Teiresias to accuse him of being the murderer of Laius. Oedipus' suspicion leads to the angry encounter with Creon and the intervention of Jocasta. In attempting to reassure Oedipus, she makes a generalization about seers: no human possesses the skill of divination. To prove her point, she recounts the oracle received by Laius, according to which he would be killed by his own son. But the human ministers of Apollo, the priestess and the priests who transmitted this oracle, were wrong. Laius was killed by robbers. As for a son, Laius had one, but he was exposed in a wilderness, with pierced ankles, within three days of his birth (707–25, cf. 853–56). Jocasta's speech, coming at about the midpoint of the drama, includes a detail which catches Oedipus' attention, and sends his investigation in a new direction, or, one might say, puts it back in the story line of the myth. Jocasta says that Laius was killed at a place where three roads meet (716). Oedipus immediately questions her about the territory in which this place is located and about other details. He fears that he is in fact the one who killed Laius. He tells the story of his youth, departure from Corinth, and consultation of the Delphic oracle concerning the identity of his parents, up to the point at which he killed an old man and all his attendants at the place described by Jocasta (771–833).

In Sophocles' version of the myth as it has unfolded so far, three points are notable. First, though Jocasta refers to the mutilation of the feet of the exposed child, neither the scars that Oedipus still bears, material evidence which her words might have pointed to, nor his name "Swollen-foot," do anything to identify him. Only later do the scars corroborate his identity after it has been all but established on other grounds (1031–36). Sophocles protracts the process of discovery, making everything depend on a reconstruction of the murder of Laius. Second, Oedipus himself has received an oracle foretelling his crimes (787–93, 994–96), an oracle which avoids answering Oedipus' question about the identity of his parents. The oracle leaves Oedipus uncertain as to who his parents are. In his mind, they might, despite the doubts that sent him to Delphi in the first place, really be Polybus and Merope in Corinth. Sophocles is the earliest source for, and perhaps the originator of, such an oracle. Oedipus' simultaneous discovery of his identity and his crimes entails not only admission of guilt but also consciousness that his attempt to thwart the prophecy has failed. His discovery thus also entails a burden of self-consciousness which the Oedipus of a Euripides or of an Antimachus, who received no oracle, does not have to bear. Though Oedipus' words "These things were Apollo" are a direct reply to the chorus' question about his self-blinding, they presuppose a recognition of the oracle's truth (1328–30). Third, when Oedipus begins to suspect that he is the murderer of Laius, his only hope of exoneration is the sole surviving eyewitness, an attendant who, according to Jocasta, spoke of robbers (715–16, 842–43). If robbers (plural), then Oedipus, who acted alone, killed not Laius but someone else.

This third point requires discussion. The nameless sole survivor, who is expected only to confirm or deny that Oedipus murdered Laius, will have a crucial role to play in Oedipus' discovery of his identity and thus of his crimes. In order to play this role, he has to have a history, which emerges in bits and pieces in non-chronological order. He was born in the house of Laius, was thus a house slave, but spent most of his life as a shepherd on Mt. Cithaeron and the environs (1123–28). He was in Laius' retinue, however, at the time when the king went to consult the oracle at Delphi, which seems to mean that he was no longer working as a shepherd (752–56, 800–813). Though Oedipus thought that he killed the whole party at the crossroads (813), the former shepherd somehow escaped and brought the news of Laius' death back to Thebes. He remained in Thebes until Oedipus arrived, having slain the Sphinx, and was made king. Then he begged Jocasta to send him back to the country and to his former work, and Jocasta obliged (758–63). From the country he now has to be summoned to give testimony about the murder of Laius (757–65). Before he arrives, a messenger comes from Corinth to report the death of Polybus.

The Corinthian messenger is the other character who has a crucial role to play in the denouement, and to him, too, Sophocles gives a history. He arrives in Thebes to report the death of Polybus, Oedipus' father, as Oedipus still believes. Half of the oracle is, then, proven wrong. Oedipus continues to fear the other half, incest with his mother. The messenger tries to reassure him. Oedipus is not in fact the son of Polybus and Merope but was brought to them by the messenger himself. As a shepherd on Mt. Cithaeron – and this is his history – he received the infant Oedipus from another shepherd, a Theban (1026–44, 1133–57). This other shepherd is the one who has already been summoned in connection with the murder of Laius. When he arrives, he reveals that the infant was the child of Laius and Jocasta, handed over to him by the latter to be destroyed. Out of pity, he spared the infant (1161–81).

The coincidence by which the Theban herdsman and the Corinthian messenger arrive at Oedipus' palace at the same time produces the discovery. This coincidence entails two others. The sole survivor of the affray at the crossroads happens to be the shepherd to whom the infant Oedipus was consigned for exposure. The messenger from Corinth happens to be the shepherd to whom the Theban handed over Oedipus. The implausibility of these double identities, the degree of intelligence, as distinguished from dogged persistence, required of Oedipus to reach the correct conclusion, and other such questions belong to the literary criticism of the play. As for the myth, one can say that Sophocles has greatly prolonged and magnified the discovery, which could be as simple as "Straightway the gods made it known amongst men," as in the *Odyssey* (cf. p. 14). Or Oedipus might at least know from early on, as in Euripides and Antimachus, that Polybus is not his father. In Aristotle's terms, what I have called the discovery is the "recognition," a fundamental component of the tragic plot, defined as the "shift from ignorance to awareness with respect to friendship and enmity" (*Poetics* 1452a30–33). His high regard for Sophocles' handling of the plot, which strongly influenced the reception of this tragedy in the Renaissance, is matter for discussion in Chapter Four.

Sophocles decisively vindicates the truth of the oracles which Laius, Jocasta, and Oedipus tried to thwart and for which Jocasta and Oedipus express scorn in the course of the tragedy. The Delphic oracle has communicated, via Apollo and his priestess and ministers, the *moira* or fate of Laius and Oedipus (376–77, 713). The point was not lost on Sophocles' contemporaries. The parodistic summary of the Oedipus story by the comic poet Aristophanes in *Frogs* (405 BC) begins: Oedipus "was wretched by nature, since, before he was born, Apollo prophesied that he would kill his father . . ." (1183–85).[17] This fate seems like an overarching necessity, superior to mortals and gods, and both Sophocles' tragedy and the myth on which it is based have often been regarded as expressions of the power of fate in this sense. Likewise, the Oedipus folktale is classified under the heading "Tales of Fate."[18] Even Freud, reflecting on *Oedipus the King*, said,

> His destiny moves us only because it might have been ours – because the oracle laid the same curse upon us before our birth as upon him. It is the fate of all of us, perhaps, to direct our first sexual impulse towards our mother and our first hatred and our first murderous impulse towards our father.[19]

But the notion that fate is the meaning of the myth and of Sophocles' tragedy is arguably reductive and trivializing. Apollo is not the agent but the prophet of Oedipus' downfall. In the theology of the Delphic oracle, Zeus knows what is fated (151). He imparts this knowledge to Apollo, who in turn speaks through his priestess at Delphi. While Sophocles vindicates the truth of the oracles received from her by the Labdacids, little or nothing that happens on stage appears to be caused directly by fate. Oedipus, who vaunts his human intelligence against the prophetic skill of Teiresias, searches for the murderer on his own, relentlessly, though he is at first misled by his suspicion of Creon, a suspicion, one might argue, arising from misdirected intelligence. This trait of Oedipus, this proud intelligence, is part of a larger hybris, seen first of all in his overreaction to the oracle which Creon brings at the beginning of the play. Oedipus, said Hölderlin (for more on whom see Ch. 5), plunges into an investigation that carries him far beyond the political responsibility entailed in the oracle's instruction concerning the plague (and indeed the plague is completely forgotten in the course of the tragedy). Then Oedipus bursts into fits of rage against Teiresias and Creon, showing on stage the temperament of the young Oedipus who killed Laius and four others in the altercation at the crossroads. He is the kind of person who might have committed these crimes even if they had not been fated.

He can be seen as the typical tyrant, playing out the tyrant's rise and fall, a pattern delineated in the *Histories* of Sophocles' contemporary, Herodotus.[20] Even if the title *Oedipus Tyrannus* was assigned by someone who only wanted to distinguish this tragedy from *Oedipus at Colonus*, it seems accurate for the play. In this perspective, Oedipus is the kind of person who, even if he had not committed the crimes, deserves to fall.

To return now to the multiple coincidences involving the Theban shepherd and the Corinthian messenger, one could regard them not as the quirks of fate but as the dramatic necessities of a tragedy which has been plotted in a certain way to bring out the simultaneous recognition and reversal which Aristotle was later to admire. Although everyone in Sophocles' contemporary audience knows what Oedipus will discover and that it will mean, at the very least, the end of his kingship, they do not know how he will make the discovery which will be his downfall. They have come to the theater to see how Sophocles will bring it about. Sophocles, one could say, makes Oedipus' fate.

Sophocles' *Oedipus at Colonus*

Prophecies always come true in folktales and myths, and the reason for their accuracy is that the outcome of the story is known.[21] From this point of view, the "fate" of Oedipus is an inference from the necessity that seems to lie in the concatenation of events in the story, a narrative necessity leading to a particular conclusion. Sophocles' *Oedipus at Colonus* provides a perfect illustration of the relation of prophecy to story line. This tragedy brings the aged Oedipus, a blind beggar long in exile from Thebes, to a town near Athens. At first, Oedipus does not know where he is. When he finds out that he is sitting in a grove of the Eumenides, he bursts into prayer:

> Queens of dread countenance, since now first at your seat
> in this land did I bend my knee,
> do not be ungracious to me and to Phoebus [Apollo],
> who, when he prophesied those many ills,
> spoke of this resting place for me after long time,

> when I came to a last region, where
> I would find a seat of the dread goddesses and a stranger's lodging . . . (84–90)

It now turns out that, when Oedipus received the prophecy concerning parricide and incest, Apollo attached a codicil, not heard of until now, that Oedipus would end his life somewhere outside of Thebes, in a place sacred to the Eumenides, who are the Erinyes in a positive aspect.[22] Teiresias, who in *Oedipus the King* was said to know "the same as Apollo" (284–85), knew that Oedipus would leave Thebes but did not know, or at least did not say, that Oedipus would end his life in a grove of the Eumenides in Colonus. The codicil to which Oedipus refers must be Sophocles' invention, in a striking application of the logic which produces prophecies from outcomes.

Did Sophocles also invent the version of the story which puts Oedipus' death in Colonus? Again, it is the question of the freedom of poets to create new versions of myths, discussed earlier in connection with Euripides. As the preceding chapter showed, Oedipus' burial somewhere outside Thebes is well attested. His death, however, as distinguished from his burial, outside of Thebes is attested only in the tragedy now under discussion and in the local historian of Attica, Androtion. If the historian's account derives from Sophocles, then the tragedy remains the sole witness to this version of the death, and Sophocles looks more like an inventor. If, on the other hand, Androtion is independent of Sophocles, then the tragedian could be regarded not as creating a new version but as working his own variation on an already existing version, as was argued in the case of Euripides. Androtion's version runs thus:

> Later, Jocasta, recognizing that she had married her son, hung herself. Oedipus, banished by Creon, came to Attica and dwelt on the so-called Hill of the Horseman [i.e., in Colonus]. And he was a suppliant in the shrine of the goddesses Demeter and Athena Poliouchos, and, when he was forcibly carried off by Creon, he had Theseus [the king of Athens] as his defender. When Oedipus was dying of old age, he called upon Theseus not to reveal his grave to any of the Thebans, for they wanted to maltreat him even as a corpse.[23]

This version differs from Sophocles' in ways that go beyond misrecollection or misunderstanding of *Oedipus at Colonus*. In Androtion, not Ismene and Antigone, as in Sophocles, but Oedipus is carried off by Creon. Creon's motive is not, as in Sophocles, to bury Oedipus near Thebes but, apparently, to maltreat him. At Colonus, Oedipus is a suppliant not of the Eumenides but of Demeter and Athena Poliouchos.[24] Further, Androtion seems to assume that Oedipus dwelt in Colonus for a considerable time before he died, whereas, in Sophocles, he dies on the day of his arrival. Androtion appears, then, to be summarizing an Attic tradition concerning the end of Oedipus' life independent of Sophocles. The existence of this parallel tradition shows that Sophocles' location of the death of Oedipus had a warrant in popular belief and that Sophocles was varying an existing narrative for his own purposes.

The specific location of Oedipus' death and burial, a grove of the Eumenides, is hardly, in the mythical and cultic tradition, a matter of chance. Sophocles does much to suggest that the Eumenides of Colonus are Erinyes. He could not call them Erinyes simply because they did not have this cult-name at Colonus, and the cult was an obscure one in any case, just as the actual grave of Oedipus, if already established at Colonus in Sophocles' time, was probably also obscure. The name Erinys is heard in the tragedy for the first time at line 1299, where Polynices blames his father for the strife between him and his brother that drove him out of Thebes: your Erinys (sing.) is the cause. Again, Polynices says that the road he must take back to the army in Argos is ill-fated thanks "to this father and his Erinyes" (1434). But the two references to the Erinys/Erinyes are quite different: the first bears on the origin of the quarrel between the brothers, the second on the doom of the army that Polynices has assembled in Argos. Polynices is certain of this doom because Oedipus has not only refused to support him – when victory will go to whichever side he supports (1332–33) – but also has cursed both his sons to death (1372–76, 1383–96). Polynices' second reference to the Erinyes of Oedipus therefore has this curse as its background.

The reason for the curse is not exactly the same as in the *Thebaid*, where it was variously the possessions of his father that Polynices set beside him and the unacceptable hip joint sent by the sons. In *Oedipus at Colonus*, the error of the sons is one of complete omission with respect to tendance. Oedipus is in exile, a beggar, and the sons have failed to provide their father with the food to keep him alive. His daughters have had to take on the role the sons should have played. (The support of Oedipus is a theme of the play.) The anger that Oedipus feels against his sons is directly the opposite of the intense love that he feels toward his daughters. The inversion of his sons' and daughters' roles has caused an emotional inversion in Oedipus, who might have been expected to value the preservation of his line above all else and thus to have cared more for his sons.

As Oedipus' anger, despite its family context, has something larger than human about it,[25] so the voice that pronounces the curse is a "divine voice" (550, 1351; cf. 1428). Indeed, the very efficacy of the curse, which is assumed by all concerned, issues not from some human capacity but from the new power that Oedipus will have as a cult partner of the Eumenides, those personified curses (for the collocation of curse, nourishment, and the Erinyes, cf. Aesch. *Sept.* 785ff.). The curse is a matter of proleptic or advance characterization: on stage, Oedipus is already the cult-hero that he will become after his death.[26] When he says farewell to his daughters, however, he becomes human for a moment. In one of the fundamental twentieth-century studies of Oedipus, "Oedipus in the Light of Folklore," Vladimir Propp wrote: "The scene of his parting from his daughters is the most moving in all tragedy. At that moment, Oedipus becomes truly human, and man enters European history."[27]

Sophocles' *Antigone*

Some of those who saw *Oedipus at Colonus*, the last of Sophocles' tragedies and the only one of his Theban tragedies which is datable (it was produced posthumously in 401 BC), had already seen Sophocles' *Antigone*. Sophocles thus alludes to this earlier tragedy when, toward the end of *Oedipus at Colonus*, Polynices, setting out on his return to Argos and the army he has assembled there, calls upon his sisters to perform the proper funeral rites for him, if his father's curse should be fulfilled and if they should return to Thebes. Polynices promises his sisters a fame that they already have (1405–10). It is Antigone alone who will bury him, however, going against the edict of Creon and paying with her life.

The stories of Oedipus' daughters are extremely various. In another version of the part of the myth dramatized by Sophocles in *Antigone*, both sisters apparently participated in the burial. The source for this version is Ion of Chios, a contemporary of Sophocles. In a lost dithyramb of his, Antigone and Ismene were burned to death by Laodamas, son of Eteocles, presumably because of their devotion to the other brother (fr. 740 *PMG*). In Euripides' lost *Antigone*, as already observed, the heroine lived on and bore a child to Haemon in secret. The seventh-century poet Mimnermus told that Tydeus killed Ismene, and the scene is attested in vase painting (fr. 21 W²).[28] Nevertheless, the sources for the versions of the myth concerning the children of Oedipus pre-dating Sophocles are insufficient to determine exactly where he stands in relation to the tradition, and the question of innovation arises, as often.

In one crucial respect, Sophocles is conservative in *Antigone*. He maintains the perspective of a multi-generational myth and of the continuous sufferings of the family. Both Antigone and the chorus see her plight against the background of the whole Labdacid myth. Reflecting on Creon's arrest of Antigone and Ismene, the chorus says: "I see the ancient pains of the house of the Labdacids heaped upon the pains of those already dead." They speak of the family's cycle of pain, from which it can find no release. "Some god comes down on them" (594–603). As Antigone is about to be led off to the underground chamber in which she will be buried alive, the chorus see her as paying for her father's misdeeds. She replies that they have touched on the most painful of her cares, and proceeds to refer to her father and the fate of the Labdacids (856–62). The conservatism of Sophocles is also reflected in his conformity with the archaic epic tradition which has Oedipus buried in Thebes. So Antigone's words presuppose (49–52).

In another respect, Sophocles is clearly innovative and eccentric. *Antigone* presupposes that the heroine, her sister and brothers are the last generation of Labdacids. The chorus regard the sisters as the last of the Labdacids (599–600). Antigone once refers to Polynices' marriage but not to his son (869–71).

OEDIPUS IN THE FOURTH CENTURY AND AFTER

The Oedipus myth continued on the tragic stage in the fourth and third centuries. Meletus, one of the accusers of Socrates, presented an *Oedipodeia* around 399 BC (the year of Socrates' death). Theodectes came into the preceding chapter apropos of the riddle of the Sphinx. Several others composed Oedipus tragedies, and a new *Antigone* is also attested (by Astydamas, 341 BC). But the name which stands out is Diogenes the Cynic. His immoralist *Oedipus*, which attached no blame to the marriage of Oedipus and Jocasta, was long remembered. Besides the new ones, the old Theban tragedies continued to be re-performed, Sophocles' *Antigone* apparently far more often than his *Oedipus*.

Tragedy is the final moment of the Oedipus myth in the history of Greek literature, the classical period of which ends, by convention, in 323 BC. Thereafter, in the Hellenistic period, neither the great nor the minor poets took Oedipus for a theme. In the genre of epigram, he and his children become handy brief references. In the longest treatment of Theban myth in this genre (eight lines), Philip, having traced the vicissitudes of Thebes, calls it a "city always pitiable" (*Anth. Pal.* 9.253.7), a totalizing view of Theban myth discernible already in the choral odes of Euripides' *Phoenician Women*. Oedipus has now become one of many items in that pitiable history. Finally, the Greek Oedipus tradition becomes something to joke about. In the first century BC, a certain Nicarchus composes an epigram in which the answer to the Sphinx's riddle is: a passive homosexual.[29]

OVERVIEW

Tragedy was the new medium for the Oedipus myth in the fifth and fourth centuries BC. Several minor tragic poets and the three major ones, Aeschylus, Sophocles, and Euripides, all wrote tragedies on the Labdacids. Aeschylus, the earliest of the three, is closest to archaic epic, putting each of the first three generations in a separate tragedy in his trilogy. The Erinys drives the action. Euripides' Theban tragedies show various peculiarities in the motifs forming the myth, and these have raised the question of innovation. Did Euripides invent these motifs?

Sophocles' three Theban tragedies sometimes raise the same kind of question. Whatever the answer, it should distinguish between fabrication out of whole cloth, on the one hand, and variation on traditional material, on the other. At the level of drama, the tendency in the tragedians is always the same, to focus on individual conflict, Oedipus with Teiresias and then Creon on the path to his discovery, Oedipus with his sons, Antigone with Creon, Polynices and Eteocles with one another. Sophocles has had greater appeal to modern audiences, probably because he was able to concentrate the action on a point of crisis at which the protagonist must know what is to be done and then do it – Oedipus when he hears the oracle about the murderer of Laius, Antigone in the face of Creon's edict, Oedipus when he learns that the hour of his death is at hand. These great achievements of dramatic imagination belong to a history which is not going to last much longer. Oedipus will disappear from the later history of Greek literature, except for brief moments, and will become the property of Latin literature for many centuries.

3

LATIN OEDIPUS: ROME AND THE MIDDLE AGES

With the Romans, Labdacid myth becomes literature in two new senses. First, Greek literature now becomes classical for the first time. Educated Romans speak and read Greek, and their culture includes the great Theban epics and tragedies of the Greek poets. In one of Cicero's philosophical dialogues, his brother Quintus speaks of his admiration for Oedipus' opening speech in *Oedipus at Colonus*.[1] Second, Romans, emulating Greek models, create a new Theban poetry. The study of the Roman Oedipus thus becomes a specifically literary project, asking about the relation between a Latin text and its Greek and sometimes also its Latin antecedents. An oral tradition independent of poetry, like the one still transmitting the Oedipus myth in the fifth and fourth centuries BC, when members of some families in Sicily and Sparta believed that they were the descendants of Oedipus, is gone, and with it the capacity of such a tradition to register oral variants in new poetic versions of the myth.

Roman comedy shows the first traces of knowledge of the Oedipus myth. In a play by Terence, in the first half of the second century BC, a slave replies to his master's reproach: *Davus sum, non Oedipus*, "I am Davus, not Oedipus," referring to Oedipus as solver of the Sphinx's riddle (*Andria* 194). The remark became proverbial. Another comic poet, Plautus, spoke of *enigmi beoti*, "Boeotian riddles" (*Poenulus* 443), i.e., riddles as difficult as the Sphinx's, creating another proverb. (Boeotia is the region of Greece in which Thebes is located.) These colloquial allusions to the riddle-solving episode suggest that the myth was widely known. Later in this century, Theban myth enters Roman

Author	Kind of work	Title(s) fr.: work survives only in fragments ti: work known by title only	Century
Accius	tragedy	none cited by title	2nd BC
Ambrose of Milan	hymn	*Hymns* (individual hymns named after first lines)	4th AD
Anon.	lament	*Planctus Oedipi*	12th AD
Anon.	mythography "Story of Oedipus"	?	?
Boccaccio	mythography	*De casibus illustrium virorum / On the misfortunes of famous men, De claris mulieribus / On famous women, Genealogie deorum gentilium / Genealogy of the pagan gods*	14th AD
Cicero	philosophical dialogue	*De finibus / On moral ends, De fato / On fate*	1st BC
Hilary of Poitiers	hymn	*Hymns* (individual hymns named after first lines)	4th AD
Hyginus	mythography	*Fabulae*	1st AD
Julius Caesar	tragedy	*Oedipus*	1st BC
Lactantius Placidus	commentary	Commentary on Statius, Thebaid	5th AD
"Lynceus"	epic	*Thebaid*	1st BC
Ovid	epic	*Metamorphoses*	1st AD
Plautus	comedy	*Poenulus*	2nd BC
Ponticus	epic	*Thebaid*	1st BC
Propertius	elegy	poems are untitled	1st BC

"Second Vatican Mythographer"	mythography	untitled	?
Seneca	tragedy	*Oedipus, Phoenician Women*	1st AD
Statius	epic	*Thebaid*	1st AD
Terence	comedy	*Andria*	2nd BC
Tertullian	Christian polemic	*Apology*	end of 2nd AD

Figure 5 Roman and medieval sources for the Oedipus myth.

tragedy on a large scale. Of Accius' forty-odd surviving titles, seven refer to Theban themes, though none is an *Oedipus*. This neglect of the Theban hero whom we consider most important has no obvious explanation but is worth pausing to reflect on. A curious fact of the Latin phase of Theban myth is that it tends to revert to the three-generational model of archaic Greek poetry. Oedipus is only one figure amongst several others.

The first Roman to compose an Oedipus tragedy was the young Julius Caesar (100–44 BC). A work of his youth, it somehow came into the possession of Augustus, who forbade its publication. Probably never read outside a small circle of Caesar's friends, it is mentioned only by Suetonius (*Jul.* 56.7). At about the time Caesar wrote his tragedy, the scholar Varro included an "Oedipothyestes" in his *Menippaean Satires* (81–67 BC), of which only a sentence survives. Varro was somehow combining the crimes of Thyestes (cannibalism) with those of Oedipus (parricide and incest), perhaps to oppose the Cynic philosopher Diogenes, who condoned them and who had written a *Thyestes*, as well as an *Oedipus* (cf. p. 55).[2]

Between Varro and Seneca (first c. AD) references to Labdacid myth are few. Early in the Augustan period, in a poem composed before 26 BC, Propertius uses Polynices and Eteocles and Jocasta interceding between them in a simile (2.9.49). The scene goes back to archaic and classical Greek works discussed in the preceding chapter, works which Romans were still reading. He addresses a poem to a certain "Lynceus," obviously a nickname, a poet who wrote a *Thebaid* (2.34.33–46). Mention of Antimachus in the lines just cited reminds again that his works continued to be available to Roman readers.

A certain Ponticus also wrote a *Thebaid*. Ovid treats pre-Labdacid stages of Theban myth – Cadmus, Actaeon, Semele, Teiresias, Bacchus, and Pentheus – in Book 3 of the *Metamorphoses*. Though he nowhere recounts the myth of Oedipus, his coinage of the massive epithet "Oedipodionian" ("of Oedipus") for Thebes shows that for him and his audience the city has become almost synonymous with Oedipus (*Met.* 15.429).

SENECA'S THEBAN TRAGEDIES

The Latin Oedipus who would reach the Middle Ages was the creation of only three works, two of them tragedies. Seneca, poet, Stoic philosopher, and advisor to Nero (ca. 1–65 AD) wrote the tragedies. His *Oedipus* takes its outline from Sophocles' *Oedipus the King*.[3] At the outset, with the plague, the return of Creon from Delphi, and the oracle, it seems as if the action will proceed as in Sophocles, and, roughly, it does. Seneca establishes the Greek model, however, only to depart from it in long stretches. He replaces Sophocles' altercation between Oedipus and Teiresias with a long description of extiscipy, divination by examination of the entrails of a sacrificial victim – in this case, two victims, a white bull and a heifer. The blind Teiresias relies on the sight of his daughter, Manto, a name known from archaic Greek epic (*Epigoni* fr. 3 Bernabé = fr. 3 Davies) but never heard in extant fifth-century Theban tragedy. Extiscipy having failed to identify the murderer of Laius, whom the oracle has directed the Thebans to discover, Teiresias turns to another procedure, necromancy, the conjuring up of the souls of the dead, in this case Laius. Creon, whom Oedipus sent to oversee the ritual, returns with Laius' reply: the king is guilty of parricide and incest. The two divinations (299–402, 530–658) and the intervening choral ode about Bacchus (Dionysus) (403–511) take up about a third of the play's 1061 lines. After the return of Creon, the tragedy stays on the tracks of the Sophoclean model, except that Jocasta commits suicide with a sword, and after, not before, the self-blinding of Oedipus. The ode just mentioned is not the only one which expands the context of this tragedy's events to a larger Theban history (and cf. the perspective of Oedipus himself, 29–31). In a tendency already noticed in the epigram of Philip (p. 55), the chorus sees Thebes as a city beset by the anger of the gods from before the time of the Labdacids (709–63).

The largest difference between Seneca and Sophocles lies in the character of the protagonist. In the prologue of the Latin tragedy, Oedipus is anything but the commanding presence he was in this place in Sophocles. The oracle that he received weighs upon him. "I am terrified by everything and I do not trust myself" (*cuncta expavesco meque non credo mihi*, 27). At this very moment, he believes, fate is devising something against him (28). Fear of fate is at the center of Seneca's *Oedipus*. The question of what Seneca meant by fate in this tragedy is exacerbated by the apparent contradiction between the chorus' doctrinaire Stoic pronouncement on the matter (*agimur fatis, cedite fatis*/"we are driven by fate, yield to fate," 980–94), on the one hand, and the destructive, one might say mythical, fate of the hero, on the other. For the reception of the Oedipus myth, the striking turn in Seneca's characterization of the hero is his fear.

Seneca's *Phoenician Women* is a 664-line fragment, which divides almost exactly into two halves. Lines 1–362 are set in the countryside outside of Thebes; the rest in the city. The first half has Sophocles' *Oedipus at Colonus* as one (probably not the only) antecedent; the second, Euripides' *Phoenician Women*. In this way, Seneca juxtaposes Oedipus the exile and Jocasta the anxious mother at the time of the campaign of the Seven. Oedipus longs for death but in a state of mind quite unlike that of his Sophoclean predecessor. He is obsessed with his guilt. He even fears that he might rape Antigone, his guide and interlocutor in this scene (50). "I flee myself" (*me fugiō*, 216). Again, as in Seneca's *Oedipus*, the hero is engaged in exploring his states of mind. A messenger comes from Thebes, asking Oedipus to intercede between his sons. He not only refuses but wishes for the destruction of Thebes and for combat between the brothers, though he does not utter a curse as such, as in archaic Greek epic and in Sophocles. Seneca construes the crimes of the Labdacids as violations of the specifically Roman virtue of *pietas*, piety in the sense of duty and respect as between members of a family. Antigone is the only exception. Of her Oedipus asks, "Can anyone born of me be pious?" (*aliquis est ex me pius?* 82). It is appropriate that it is Antigone who labels the war between the brothers "impious" (290). Oedipus, scorning the messenger, asks, "Am I the one to teach law and pious love?" (330–31).

Antigone, somehow back in Thebes, encourages her mother to forestall the battle (403–6, 414–18). She dashes between the two armies, causes them to halt, and makes an impassioned speech: "If you decide on piety [*pietas*, 455], give up the war for your mother." The play breaks off at the point at which Jocasta seems to have persuaded Polynices to desist. She says that Eteocles will pay any price for power, and his reign will itself be his punishment (645–64).

STATIUS' *THEBAID*

The third work which was to carry Oedipus on to the Middle Ages was the *Thebaid* by Statius (ca. 45–ca. 96 AD). The *Thebaid* is an epic poem in twelve books on the war between Eteocles and Polynices, the sons of Oedipus, over the kingship of Thebes. In the history of Greek and Latin literature, it is one of several *Thebaids* but the only complete one.

In the first book, Statius takes the "troubled house of Oedipus" (*Oedipodae confusa domus*, 16) as his theme, and begins with Oedipus, who is described as dwelling in an underground chamber (49–50). He curses his sons for their neglect and contempt of him (56–87). Tisiphone, one of the Erinyes, hears him, and goes to Thebes, where Eteocles and Polynices are immediately struck by the "family madness" (*gentilis furor*, 126). In twelve books, Statius narrates the war between them over the kingship of Thebes. As if Tisiphone were not enough, Laius appears to Eteocles in a dream, baring the wound in his throat and pouring blood on him. Eteocles takes the warning and springs into action (2.120–33). Laius appears again in Book 4 (604–45), thanks once again (as in Seneca) to the necromancy of Teiresias, who wishes to learn the outcome of the war which is about to start. Antigone watches from the walls as the battle is about to begin and receives from Laius' former armor-bearer a detailed commentary on the seven chiefs of the invading army (7.244–373). She and Ismene accompany Jocasta, now alive, though she was apparently already dead in the prologue (1.72), into the Seven's camp. Jocasta almost persuades Polynices to return with her and negotiate with Eteocles.

Tydeus stops him, and the Erinys seizes her moment (7.470–563). Menoeceus, Creon's son, commits suicide, sacrificing himself to save the city (10.756–82), an episode drawn from Euripides' *Phoenician Women* (cf. p. 38).

Oedipus reappears twice in the poem after Book 1. In Book 8, during a lull in the fighting, those in Thebes celebrate a temporary success, and, for the first time since his self-blinding and withdrawal from the world, Oedipus attends a banquet, accompanied by Antigone. He pretends to support Eteocles; he really only wants to hear more about the war (240–58). In Book 11, after his sons have killed each other, Oedipus, led by Antigone, goes out onto the battlefield, casts himself upon their corpses, and expresses remorse (580–633). (The scene will have repercussions in the Middle Ages.) Jocasta commits suicide upon the sword of Laius (634–47).

In the twelfth and final book, the widows and mothers of the slain soldiers in Polynices' armies come from Thebes. They learn from a survivor that Creon has denied burial and are advised to seek the aid of Theseus, king of Athens (105–76). Here Statius is harking back to Euripides' *Suppliants* (cf. p. 38). Argeia, the wife of Polynices, detaches herself from the others and makes her way to her husband's corpse (177–348). Antigone comes out of the city, also in search of Polynices. She joins with Argeia. They drag his corpse to a still-burning Theban pyre. It proves to be Eteocles', and the movement of the logs and the division of the flames show that the conflict between the brothers is continuing post mortem (349–446). The role of Argeia here, unprecedented, is perhaps Statius' invention. (It is the same old question, the one raised earlier in connection with Euripides [p. 39].) The Argive women go to Athens and secure the aid of Theseus, who marches forthwith to Thebes. In a short battle, he kills Creon, before he can execute Antigone and Argeia, and ensures the burial of the slain Argives (540–796).

What is Theban myth about in Statius? Tisiphone, whose baleful influence pervades the poem, is no longer the chain-reaction Erinys of, say, Aeschylus' Theban trilogy, originating and operating on the human plane, but stands for a more abstract, cosmic force, on a Stoic model, which will play itself out in the events of the epic. Thebes, called "guilty" in the opening lines, in accordance with a vision of the city which goes back at least to the choral odes of Euripides' *Phoenician Women*, will see the mad anger of the Labdacids finally exhaust itself in the mutual slaughter of Eteocles and Polynices.[4] With Theseus, a new world, again on a Stoic model, can begin.

OEDIPUS IN THE MIDDLE AGES

The situation of a double inheritance of Theban poetry, Greek and Latin, was not destined to last. Knowledge of ancient Greek began to die out in the waning Roman Empire, disappearing first in the provinces. Already in the fourth century AD, Greek ceased to be the language of the liturgy in the Western church and was replaced by Latin. Hilary of Poitiers and Ambrose of Milan wrote the first Latin hymns in this century. Augustine describes how painful it was for him in his school days in north Africa to study Greek grammar, and he never became proficient in this language. He had to rely on translations of the Greek Christian authors.[5] With the barbarian invasions of Italy and the removal of the last Roman emperor (476 AD), the school system collapsed, and the study of Greek came to an end. From the fifth century onwards, even the Latin writers who exhibit a good knowledge of Greek texts may not have read them in the original. For about a thousand years, no one in Western Europe, except in isolated pockets, read Sophocles or any other Greek text. It was thanks to Seneca and Statius, especially the latter, that knowledge of the Oedipus myth lived on. As the numbers and distribution of manuscripts show, the epic poet was read far more than the tragedian.[6]

The Christian theologian Tertullian (ca. 160–ca. 240) spoke of Seneca as "often our side" (*saepe noster, Apology* 20), and Seneca was believed to have been a correspondent of the Apostle Paul. A collection of their (spurious) letters was in circulation.[7] These medieval opinions concerning Seneca ought to have justified the reading of his tragedies, and, in certain places, they did. But not in many. It was Seneca the philosopher, "moral Seneca" as Dante calls him (*Inferno* Canto 4.141), whom medieval readers appreciated. The discovery of a new manuscript of Seneca by the early humanist Lovato de Lovati (1241–1309) in Padua was a turning point in the fortune of Seneca's tragedies. This manuscript contained notes and metrical explanations which, for the first time, allowed a medieval reader to read a tragedy as tragedy. Working at the same time as Lovato but independently, the English Dominican Nicholas Trevet wrote a commentary on Seneca's tragedies (1308–21). The upsurge of interest in Seneca is reflected in Boccaccio (1313–75), who shows knowledge of his *Oedipus* (see below).[8]

Statius was the favorite among medieval readers. He appears in Cantos 21–22 of Dante's *Purgatory*, where he says that, though baptized, he remained a secret Christian, and it is because of his tepid faith that he has now been dwelling in Purgatory for several centuries. In the mid-twelfth century, an unknown French poet modernized the *Thebaid* in the new romance style. The *Roman de Thèbes* proliferated into three versions (represented by five surviving manuscripts) so independent of one another that modern editorial technique cannot recreate the original. The last attempt to establish an ur-text occurred at the end of the nineteenth century.[9] The *Thebaid* also inspired a popular song, "Planctus Oedipi" ("Lament of Oedipus"), known from fifteen manuscripts, some of which contain a musical setting (discussed below). Medieval commentary on the *Thebaid* was another source of knowledge of Oedipus. Around 400 AD, Lactantius Placidus wrote a preface to the first book of the *Thebaid*, in which he recounted the life of Oedipus, and this introduction quite probably provided the poet of the *Roman de Thèbes* with his preface, of over 500 lines, on the same subject.[10]

This preface, long considered lost, and known only from the author's reference to it in his comment on Book 1, line 61, has now perhaps appeared in two different manuscripts, detached from the commentary. Whatever scholars decide about the authenticity of these passages, it is clear that the original preface provided what might be called the standard medieval life of Oedipus. The preface was the source not only for the poet of the *Roman de Thèbes* but also for the life of Oedipus found in a Vatican manuscript (of the anonymous "Second Vatican Mythographer"), in an anonymous "Story of Oedipus" in a Milan manuscript, in the Old Irish *Togail Tebe*/*Destruction of Thebes*, and in Boccaccio's *Genealogie deorum gentilium*/*Genealogy of the pagan gods*.[11] These texts have several common features which set them apart from the Greek and Roman

versions of the Oedipus myth. The servants who expose the infant
Oedipus hang him from a tree by his feet (fig. 6). The rescuer of
Oedipus is Polybus. The ancient physiognomy of the Sphinx is now
forgotten, and she – or he – has become a vaguely visualized *monstrum*
(fig. 7).[12] The identity of Oedipus is discovered when Jocasta sees the
scars on his feet (fig. 8). This story, sometimes combined with other
sources, sometimes the *Roman de Thèbes* itself, was passed on to
another generation of medieval writers. In one respect, the motif of
Oedipus hanging by his feet from a tree, it survived the Renaissance,
defied modern scholarship, and became part of the Oedipus myth
as known to the twentieth century. This form of the exposure of
Oedipus turns up in both André Gide's and Jean Cocteau's Oedipus
dramas.

Oedipus was also known under other names. The medieval stories
of Judas and of Pope Gregory, told in popular legends, poetry, and
sermons, bear a close resemblance to the story of Oedipus. Though
the question of their historical relationship to ancient sources for

Figure 6 Oedipus discovered hanging by his feet. Medieval manuscript. Princeton
Garrett MS 128, fol. 4v. Courtesy of Princeton University Library.

Figure 7 Oedipus and the Sphinx. Medieval manuscript in Bibliothèque Nationale, Paris. Bibliothèque nationale de France.

Figure 8 Jocasta identifies Oedipus by scars on his feet. Medieval manuscript. Morgan Library, G. 23, fol. 9v.

Oedipus is difficult, it seems certain that they lie outside the transmission of the story via Statius and commentary on Statius. Judas and Pope Gregory are discussed further on in this chapter.

Roman de Thèbes

The anonymous poet (or poets) of this, the first courtly romance, may or may not have directly used Statius. A summary of the *Thebaid* is sometimes posited as the source. The poet(s) certainly used Lactantius Placidus' preface to Book 1 of Statius (discussed above) for the life of Oedipus with which the poem begins. In any case, the new poem omits much of Statius in order to concentrate on feats of arms, love, and the intricacies of feudal obligations. It exults in descriptions of beautiful clothes and furnishings and of course beautiful women. Ismene and Antigone wear the latest styles of the twelfth century AD. The secret Christianity of Statius for the most part remains a secret, however, in the transposition of the *Thebaid* into the romance. The poem skillfully subdues Christian (and, for that matter, also pagan) religious reference. Mention of Christ, the Virgin Mary, or saints (except in place names) is lacking.[13] The main exception to this rule is Ismene's decision, following the death of her lover, Ates, to found an abbey and to become a nun (6471–508). The poem also describes marvels like the pet tigress who could drink a copper cauldron full of wine (4284–302). It recounts, besides the love of Ates and Ismene, that of Eteocles and Salamandre, and that of Parthenopaeus and Antigone, relationships that would not have occurred to Statius in his wildest dreams. Long new episodes are added, for example, the one concerning Daire le Roux/Darius the Red (900 to 2500 lines depending on the version of the poem), which combines, in large doses of each, feudal legalisms and courtly romance.[14]

   In this episode, a young knight, a Theban, is captured by Polynices, who bribes him, with the promise of land, to return, as a hostage, to the city and arrange for the surrender of his father's tower. His father, Darius the Red, cannot agree to this act of treason, though he holds that all those in Thebes, the supporters of Eteocles, are already treasonous, with respect to the compact as originally negotiated between the two brothers. Darius' son returns to Polynices, taking various gifts, which include a cup with a cover in which a topaz knob is set, "just as the book by Statius said" (7820–24). But Darius is not found in Statius nor is a topaz knob, as the sly poet probably knew. The following day, at the court of Eteocles, Darius expresses an opinion on the illegality of Eteocles' position vis-à-vis his brother and advises compromise. The counsel of Darius infuriates Eteocles, who strikes the baron on the head with a stick. Darius now, in his mind, has full right to avenge himself. He sends word to his son that he will give up his tower, which Polynices now occupies. Eteocles besieges the tower. His forces capture it, along with Darius, who is led in chains before Eteocles. Though ready to execute Darius on the spot, he is persuaded to hear his barons debate the case. A certain Otes speaks for Darius; Creon against him. Off to one side, Jocasta advises her son that it is in his best interest to spare Darius. Antigone then comes to her brother with a stronger argument: she brings Darius' daughter, whom Eteocles has long courted in vain. Jocasta explains the terms: return father to daughter, and she will be your lover. Eteocles accepts, though his official position is that he has accepted the advice of his barons, a majority of whom side with Otes. Darius is free. The episode would be over, except that the son of Darius is still in Polynices' hands. The army demands his execution but Polynices "acted as a noble man" (8597) and released the young man. So ends the episode.

What is Theban myth about in the *Roman de Thèbes*? Erich Auerbach's generalization applies well to this poem in particular: "A self-portrayal of feudal knighthood with its mores and ideals is the fundamental purpose of the courtly romance."[15] The conflict between Eteocles and Polynices, as given in Statius, offered the possibility not only of evolving various romances, but also of exploring, in feudal terms, the original compact between the brothers and the complex relations between them and their various retainers.

From Statius and Seneca to Boccaccio and beyond

Giovanni Boccaccio used Theban myth again and again in his Latin works. In his *De casibus illustrium virorum/On the misfortunes of famous men* (1355–74), he draws on both Lactantius Placidus' preface to Statius and also on Seneca's *Oedipus,* and thus demonstrates a working knowledge of the Roman tragedian, though not in the genre of tragedy. His shorter account of Oedipus in *De claris mulieribus/On famous women* (1360–74) is consistent with the one in the work on famous men. In his *Genealogie* (1350? to the end of his life), he relies heavily on the lost preface, and there is nothing that must have come from Seneca.

A version in French prose of Boccaccio's *De Casibus Virorum Illustrium* by Laurence de Premierfait provided John Lydgate with the material for his *Fall of Princes* (composed in the 1430s). It consists of 36,365 lines of which 686 (3158–843) tell the story of the Labdacids from the time of Oedipus' birth to the deaths of his sons. Lydgate of course has the shepherd take pity on the infant Oedipus and hang him by his feet from a tree –

> Took first a knyff, & did his besi peyne
> Thoruhout his feet to make holis tweyne.
>
> Took a smal rod off a yong oseer,
> Perced the feet, allas, it was pite! –
> Bynd him faste, and bi good leiseer
> The yonge chld he heeng vpon a tre,
> Off entent that he ne sholde be
> Thoruh wilde beestis, cruel & sauage,
> Been sodenli deuoured in ther rage. (3240–48)
>
> [He] took first a knife, and did his utmost
> To make twin holes through his feet.
>
> [He] took a small branch from a young osier,
> pierced the feet – alas, it was a pity! –
> bound him fast, and deliberately
> he hung the young child upon a tree,
> with the intention that he should not be
> by wild beasts, cruel and savage,
> not be suddenly devoured in their rage.

What the Theban episode as a whole provides is, as the title of the poem predicts, a lesson for princes and princesses. It is that kingdoms divided by internecine struggle cannot endure. Also, rulers should cherish their subjects. The events of Oedipus' life also show fortune's vicissitudes (3277–97) and remind, through the riddle of the Sphinx, that death awaits all men (3424–65). In this way, royalty learns that it is only human.

Lydgate also wrote a *Siege of Thebes* (in the period 1420–1422). It is 4716 lines long, in three parts after the prologue (1–176): foundation of Thebes by Amphion (177–1046); disputes of Eteocles ("Ethiocles") and Polynices ("Polymyte") and their agreement to an annual alternating kingship (1047–2552); the campaign of the Seven (2553–4716). Lydgate's main source is a French prose redaction of the *Roman de Thèbes*. Six relatively short passages (the longest about fifty lines) come from Boccaccio's *Genealogie*. The force of the medieval French romance continues strong. But what is Theban myth about in the *Siege of Thebes*? Lydgate, as in the *Fall of Princes*, takes the myth as the occasion for admonitions to kings and princes. He is the champion of the humble and oppressed.[16]

Planctus Oedipi ("Lament of Oedipus")

The anonymous twelfth-century *Planctus* belongs to the popular medieval genre of the lament for sin.[17] It seizes upon the one place in ancient literature in which Oedipus shows regret for his curse on his sons, the passage in Book 11 of Statius' *Thebaid* cited above (p. 63). The *Planctus* consists of twenty-one mono-rhymed quatrains, in which the third and fourth lines usually repeat and paraphrase the sense of the first two. In this way, the repentance of Oedipus takes on an obsessive quality. The poem begins:

> diri patris | infausta pignora,
> ante ortus | damnati tempora,
> quia vestra | sic iacent corpora,
> mea dolent | introrsus pectora.

> Unfortunate children of an abominable father,
> damned before the time of your birth,
> because your bodies thus lie here,
> my heart grieves within.

The regular caesura or word-break after the first four syllables (marked in the quotation above) adds to the effect of obsession conveyed by the insistent repetition of rhyme and sense.

For the most part, suppressing Christian reference, the poet tries to portray Oedipus as a penitent pagan, but the genre was in itself a Christian one. There were laments of Peter, Mary Magdalene, and Isidore, bishop of Seville, amongst others. The generic affiliations of the "Lament of Oedipus" would have predisposed its audience to a Christian understanding of the pagan hero's repentance. Already in its second line ("damned before the time of your birth"), the poem may allude to Original Sin. This line may also refer to the curse on the family of Oedipus, which goes back to the murder of Laius or even further to Pelops' curse on Laius. Or it may refer both to the curse and to Original Sin. While the medieval poet refrains from explicit reference, a Christian conception surfaces in such lines as

> me infami rerum luxuria
> infernalis foedavit furia.
>
> me with the infamous excess of the world
> the infernal fury has stained.

While "excess" (i.e., sensuous excess) does not correspond to anything in the ancient Oedipus myth, it could be a medieval Christian allusion to Oedipus' incestuous marriage. *Luxuria* was of course one of the Seven Deadly Sins. At the same time, the medieval poet, with *furia*, maintains fidelity to his source, Statius (cf. Stat. *Theb.* 1.68, 73; 11.619). One has, then, already in the twelfth century, the amalgam of Christian and pagan which recastings of the Oedipus myth will later show again and again.

Though it can be argued that the contrite Oedipus of the "Planctus" has been Christianized, the fact remains that he is the son who killed his father and the father whose curse killed his sons. He is the bad son and the bad father. As the bad son, he is the opposite of Christ, and the comparison between the two, negative for Oedipus, may also be implicit in the poem. It was to be rendered explicit when Christian theology had to deal with Freud and psychoanalysis.[18]

Judas and Pope Gregory

In the stories of Judas and Gregory, originating in the same period as the "Planctus," the Middle Ages could see the juxtaposition of *desperatio*, despair, and *poenitentia*, penance. These were the fundamental alternatives for the Christian asking how he could bear his guilt. One of the forms in which these two stories were told was the popular legend, Gregory's belonging to the genre of the saint's legend. In the case of Judas, for whom the Bible provided no biography before the point at which he became a disciple of Christ, the myth of Oedipus came into play. Of the two main versions of the Judas legend, one has his shins mutilated when he is exposed as a child. This mutilation suggests knowledge, direct or indirect, of Lactantius Placidus' preface to the first book of the *Thebaid*. The other form is distinguished by the anachronistic figure of Pilate (who is assumed to be governor of Judaea already when Judas is a young man, i.e., long before 26 AD, the year in which Pilate became governor), by exposure of the child on water (as in modern folktales of the Oedipus type), and its rescue by a queen. The main innovation in the Judas legend, however, which occurs in both versions, is the trespasser's parricide, as it can be called. Judas enters his father's orchard or garden as a thief, meets resistance, and kills his father, of whose identity he is unaware. After his discovery of his crimes, he joins Jesus, and, after the betrayal, hangs himself.

An anonymous life of Judas from a twelfth-century Latin manuscript runs as follows:

> I have composed the life of Judas the betrayer, who was evil in his origin, worse in his life, and worst of all in his end. Now his father, so far as he had repute amongst men, was of abundant means and esteemed honorable in the eyes of all his neighbors. One night he saw in a vision that he had a son who threatened him

with death (for his wife was now pregnant) – the son from whom this deceitful trick was to come. When, however, the child was born, the father, reflecting upon and feeling terror at such an omen, pierced its shins and exposed it in underbrush rather far from the city of Jerusalem. Certain shepherds, hearing its wailing and weeping, took it from the place, and bringing it to Scariot, caused it to be nursed by a certain woman. Nourished and grown to manhood, he attached himself to King Herod and mingling with his servants he served the king and the soldiers with complete honesty. And yet, as is the custom of servants, he gave out lavishly whatever he had and kept as much as possible for himself. It happened, however, that once Herod held a ceremonial banquet with the nobles in Jerusalem and, amongst dishes of many sorts, the king sought fresh fruit. Hastening to satisfy the king's desire and going into his father's orchard (he did not know it was his father's), by force he plucked the fruit and stripped the trees bare. The man whose property this was, in high dudgeon and full of bitterness, pitted himself against the upstart, but Judas, prevailing, struck and killed him. The whole city was stirred up against Judas and, falling upon him, determined to put him to death. But Judas, fleeing to Herod's protection, escaped the danger of death. Herod, himself frightened, proceeded in such a way that Judas might win forgiveness from the friends of the murdered man, lest, because of a single crime, he pass on to some greater risk. Taking counsel, therefore, Herod joined Judas to the wife of the murdered man, he himself and everyone else ignorant that she was his mother. One day it happened that Judas appeared nude before his mother and wife, and when she saw the scars of the wounds on his shins, she suspected that it was her own son, whom she had once abandoned, cast out in the underbrush. Thus, she asked him who his father was, who his mother was, who his parents were, and whence, from what province, he sprang, by whom he had been reared. He said that he did not know but had heard only this from his nurse, that the had been thrown out in that place in the underbrush, found by shepherds, brought to Scariot, and raised there. And that when he had reached manhood, he had joined the servants of Herod and had pleased many with his services. Hearing this she collapsed and, crying out that she was wretched, said, "Unfortunate the vision of my husband, which has been fulfilled by the son and moreover the madness of the sin and malice redounds to me. May the day of my birth perish and may the darkness of the shadows cover him over." Judas, however, perceiving that he had committed such a villainy, felt remorse, and, penitent at such a crime, left his mother. But at that time Jesus was dwelling in those places, who by his preaching and aid healed the bodies of many and recalled their minds from many sins. Those who came to him weighed down with many sins he took to himself and like a shepherd he rescued from attack sheep snatched from the jaws of wolves. Perceiving his virtue and piety, Judas went to him and asked that Jesus take pity on him. Jesus agreed to his desire, and also allowed Judas to stay with him among his disciples. Jesus even entrusted what he had to Judas, that he might provide the necessities of life to him and the others. He held the purse strings and stole what he could. And what the design of Judas was appeared in the end, because he sold his master for a price and betrayed him to the Jews. At last he hanged himself and ended his life with a wretched death. But you, Lord, have mercy on us. He who perseveres in good until the end shall be saved.[19]

This life of Judas, one of dozens in medieval Latin, is of the type which is clearly in touch with Lactantius Placidus' life of Oedipus.

The Gregory legend differs from the ancient Oedipus myth and from the Judas legend in two main respects. The incestuous origin of the hero is the reason for his exposure. He does not commit parricide. In his repentance and eventual exaltation to the office of pope, his story resembles the phase of the ancient myth dramatized in *Oedipus at Colonus.*

Comparison with modern folktales of the Oedipus type shows that the legends of Judas and of Gregory are not as different as they seem.[20] In twenty-seven of these folktales, the trespasser's parricide is inverted and becomes the watchman's parricide. The hero, who has returned in one way or another to his parents' home, has found employment. His father sets him to guard the orchard or garden, and, in the line of duty, son kills father by mistake. In these folktales, in which the degree of guilt attaching to the parricide is diminished, the hero is often forgiven in the end. The basic pattern, which is the pattern of Sophocles' *Oedipus the King* and *Oedipus at Colonus* taken together, consists of crimes (and the events which made them possible), penance or suffering, and forgiveness. It is well illustrated in the legend of St. Andrew of Crete (ca. 660–740), which is attested only in modern versions but is undoubtedly earlier.

These versions explain the origin of his Canon of Repentance.[21] ("Canon" here refers to an ode or hymn sung in the services of the Eastern church. St. Andrew was believed to have introduced the use of such canons.) He is an even better example than Gregory of the extremes of sin and penance. In one of the folktales, having been exposed as an infant with a wound on his belly, he is rescued by a nun and then raised in her convent. Beginning at age fifteen, he began to seduce or rape the 300 nuns in this convent, one by one, including the Mother Superior. Andrew is of course expelled. He proceeds to kill his father and marry his mother. His mother, having recognized the scar on his belly, sends him to "the city of Crete" to find a confessor. On the way, he murders the three priests who refuse to forgive him. He goes to the bishop, who summons his mother. The bishop gives them spiritual instruction and then puts Andrew in an underground cell. There he prayed, lamented his sins, and wrote the Canon of Repentance. The bishop placed a lock in his mother's nostrils, threw the key into the sea, and sent her off to a life of wandering and praising God. After thirty years, she returned to the place of her son's penance. At this time, the bishop found the key in a fish that was served to him for a meal. He removed the lock in the mother's nostrils and tonsured her into an order of nuns. He then released Andrew from his cell. "And then the bishop praised God and Our Lord Jesus Christ that Andrew was vouchsafed to accept forgiveness of his sins, and the bishop tonsured Andrew into monkshood." He then introduced the canon into the services of the church. In a few days, the bishop died and Andrew succeeded him.[22]

The Christian Oedipus

The common theme in these medieval recastings of the figure of Oedipus is repentance and redemption, which is the central theme of Christian theology. The Oedipus story thus serves, as it did in the past and as it will do again in the future, to articulate the most profound concerns of the culture in which it is retold. It does so by representing the Oedipus figure as attaining the worst and/or the best possible outcome.

Christ's sacrifice is not a completely free gift but requires repentance on the part of the sinner. Though the Sacrament of Penance, dating from the early centuries of the church, varied enormously in severity from place to place and from time to time, the penitent always had to confess his sin, to be genuinely contrite, and to undergo some kind of physical discipline. The medieval story of Gregory illustrates the efficacy of penance thus conceived.[23] Even someone who has committed incest can be forgiven and not only forgiven: he can become pope. Because Gregory had the capacity not only for the greatest sin but also for the most extreme penance, he attained the highest rank in the Christian church.

Judas, however, having committed the same crimes, does not repent and is not forgiven. "At last he hanged himself and ended his life with a wretched death," to quote the end of one of the medieval lives of Judas. Another says that "he hung himself in despair."[24] Despair is a sin. In Prudentius' *Psychomachia*, it is represented by suicide. In Giotto's *Last Judgment* in the Church of S. Maria dell'Arena at Padua, the figure of Desperatio (Despair) hangs herself. "Judas dies without ever being aware of his place in the divine plan of salvation, just before the saving death of the Redeemer. He is perhaps the last man to die under the Old Law, before the dawning of the Age of Grace. Gregorius, by contrast, lives after the first Pentecost, when salvation was made known to the world. . . ." Indeed, "if the warning against despair . . . is so insistent in all the Gregorius texts, it is because they are rooted in the memory of Judas."[25]

FUTURE OF THE MEDIEVAL OEDIPUS

The stories of Judas and Gregory lived on into modern times in oral tradition. So did other folktales, presumably just as old, with differently named protagonists but the same story pattern. These modern folktales are the basis of the Oedipus folktale type, discussed in the introduction to this book. The discipline of folklore studies tells the story of this story.[26] If, however, one tracks versions of the myth in which the protagonist is named "Oedipus," one follows Statius, his medieval recastings, and the tragedian Seneca of the later Middle Ages on into the Renaissance. Now the literary history of the Oedipus myth becomes more complex, as Greek tragedy is rediscovered.

OVERVIEW

The Roman Oedipus, as he was to reach the Middle Ages and Renaissance, was the creation of only three works: two tragedies by Seneca and an epic by Statius, all of the first century AD Statius' poem was already a recasting of the Greek Thebaids, which he could still read (as we cannot) in their entirety, with which he combined numerous borrowings from Greek tragedy. This highly sophisticated work then underwent another recasting in the form of a medieval romance, the *Roman de Thèbes*. Seneca's *Oedipus* did not have the same fortune in the Middle Ages. It was rediscovered rather late, and, even then, it could only be a source text for works in other genres. There was no medieval tragedy, thus no medieval recasting of Seneca's tragedy. A passage in Statius' epic inspired a song crystallizing the issue of repentance which the medieval mind could see in the Oedipus myth. Likewise, the legends of Judas and Pope Gregory yield Christian morals to what is recognizably the story pattern of the Oedipus myth: the sin of despair and the efficacy of penance.

OEDIPUS AFTERWARDS

4

REDISCOVERY OF SOPHOCLES: FROM THE RENAISSANCE TO THE EIGHTEENTH CENTURY

Knowledge of ancient Greek returned to Western Europe via Italy, which, especially through the Venetians, had extensive contacts with the Greek-speaking Byzantine Empire. It was a Byzantine diplomat who offered the first regular introduction to ancient Greek in Italy. The place was Florence and the year was 1397, a key date in the history of Renaissance humanism.[1] Knowledge of the language led to a demand for manuscripts of ancient Greek authors. The Sicilian Aurispa, a scholar and entrepreneur, brought the first copy of Sophocles to Italy in 1417. But the number of persons who could read Sophocles or any other Greek author remained small. Humanists acquired knowledge of the ancient language with difficulty, lacking an adequate number of teachers and even a grammar. The situation began to change when Constantinople fell to the Ottomans in 1453. A stream of refugees came to Italy, and some taught their native language in order to earn a living. For Sophocles and other Greek authors to become standard reading, one more thing was necessary, the new technology of printing. Aldus Manutius (1449–1515) established the first viable printing house for Greek texts in Venice at the end of the fifteenth century. He published the first edition of Sophocles in 1502–04.[2]

OEDIPUS IN ITALY

The uptake of the Greek tragedian was immediate and persistent. In the course of the sixteenth century in Italy, there appeared in print as many as ninety-one editions and translations of Sophocles. Forty-four works, nearly all translations and commentaries, exist in manuscript, unpublished. As against this total of 135 for Sophocles, Aeschylus shows thirty. This eager reception did not occur in a vacuum. Italy saw, on the average, a new tragedy every year in this century, with a vast parallel output of drama criticism and treatises on tragedy. It has rightly been called one of the ages of tragedy in Western history.[3]

The numbers for Sophocles help to correct the impression that Seneca was the main influence on humanist tragedy. Seneca came first in the sense that the first edition of his tragedies was published by Andreas Gallicus of Ferrara in ca. 1474–75, a quarter of a century before the first edition of Sophocles. That the influence of Seneca in Italy and elsewhere in Europe was profound no one would deny. Erasmus' edition (1515) is a good example. The present chapter attempts to restore the balance, for the sixteenth century, between Seneca and Sophocles by highlighting the latter and his *Oedipus the King* in particular. We will see that, in the next century, the Sophoclean model is the one that becomes determining for French neoclassical drama.

The newly discovered Sophocles had the powerful support of Aristotle, whose *Poetics* came to dominate both literary theory and the practical criticism of tragedy in the sixteenth century. In this work, Aristotle mentions *Oedipus the King* more often than any other tragedy, and he takes it as an example of the finest plot-construction. Bernard Weinberg has described Aristotle's effect on humanist criticism as follows: "The problem for the critic was to start from the new play as he found it, to extract from it the theoretical presuppositions on which it must have been based, to test these against his own reading of the *Poetics* to see if they were genuinely Aristotelian, and then to judge the excellence of the play."[4]

The *Poetics* was known in Western Europe from a relatively early date, but had to make several starts. William of Moerbeke (ca. 1215–86), a Dominican posted to Thebes, amongst other places in Greece, learned Greek and translated much of Aristotle, including the

Poetics (1278), into Latin. But the time for its literary influence lay far in the future. Giorgio Valla produced a reasonably accurate translation of the *Poetics* in 1498, though Averroës' Arabic commentary, translated into Latin by Hermannus Alemannus in 1481, continued to be read. Manutius published the Greek text in 1508, the turning point for the history of the *Poetics* in Europe. A new edition of the Greek text by Alessandro de' Pazzi, with a Latin version, became the standard (1536), and Francesco Robortello published the first major commentaries on the *Poetics* in 1548. Aristotle gradually supplanted Horace as the authority on tragedy for the sixteenth century, as Sophocles supplanted Seneca as the model for Oedipus tragedy.

The dominance of Aristotle meant the dominance of Sophocles' *Oedipus the King* as the model for tragedy. In fact, Aristotle and Sophocles' tragedy sometimes appear together as two sides of the same critical canon. After a public reading of his tragedy, *Didone* (1543), Giovambattista Giraldi Cinzio had to answer a series of objections. Some of these referred directly to Aristotle; one to *Oedipus the King*, "from which," said the anonymous critic, "Aristotle drew the precepts as from the true idea of tragedy." Again, Bartolomeo Cavalcanti could object to Sperone Speroni's *Canace* on the twin charges that it departed from the best model, Sophocles, and that it departed from the precepts of Aristotle. The closeness of Sophocles and Aristotle in the mind of the sixteenth century is illustrated by the remark of a certain Giacomo Dolfini concerning *Oedipus the King*: "it is enough to say this alone, that it springs from the Genius of Sophocles and the Idea of tragedy taught by Aristotle."[5]

Two impulses drive reception

Two impulses drive reception of Greek texts and of *Oedipus the King* in particular in the sixteenth century. One is philological interest in the original, shown in the first place in the printed editions, which required decisions about manuscript authority (humanist editors typically consulted two manuscripts and three at the most). Commentaries and translations supported the new editions. Humanists lectured on Sophocles in Italian universities. Demetrius Chalcondyles, who had taught Greek in various Italian universities in the last quarter of the preceding century, lectured on Sophocles in Milan in 1502–3, the very years in which Manutius' edition of the poet was appearing.[6] Alessandro de' Pazzi, whose *Poetics* has already been mentioned, made the first translation of *Oedipus the King* into Italian in 1524–25. Outside Italy, the same impulses are at work. Enthusiasm for new editions of the Greek text of Sophocles is symptomatic. That of Adrianus Turnebus (Adrien Tournèbe) appeared in Paris in 1552–53; that of Henricus Stephanus (Henri Estienne) in 1568. That of the Dutchman Willem Canter (1579) was to remain a standard for more than two centuries.[7]

The other impulse is creative imitation. In 1560, Giovanni Andrea dell' Anguillara produced his own version of *Oedipus the King* at Vicenza in a wooden theater designed by Palladio. He introduced into Sophocles elements from Seneca and from Euripides' *Phoenician Women*. For the meaning of the drama, the most important change which Anguillara makes with respect to his primary model is in the ending. He follows Euripides in having Oedipus live on past the battle of his sons and the suicide of Jocasta over their corpses. This large amplification of Sophocles' tragedy has to be understood in relation to Oedipus' response to the plague at the beginning of the play: unlike the Sophoclean Oedipus, this Oedipus reflects that he, too, could die and he therefore makes his testament. He leaves Thebes to Eteocles (the elder son in this version) and Corinth to Polynices. At the end, Oedipus has come to know that he is not the son of the king of Corinth and has no throne there to bequeath and that he is only the usurper, through murder of his predecessor (his father), of the throne of Thebes. Oedipus' tragedy is thus his fall from power and his failure to preserve the kingship of the city in his own line.[8]

Another notable adaptation of Theban myth is that of Ludovico Dolce. In his *Giocasta* (1560), he translates and rewrites *Phoenician Women*. Fate and fortune control all outcomes, which humans can never foresee. Under these conditions, the ambition for power is senseless, as Jocasta tells her sons. Kings will fall. Dolce, who did not know Greek, was working from a Latin translation of Euripides. An anecdote about the future of Dolce's play outside Italy shows how quickly the activities of the Italian humanists reverberated elsewhere in Europe. In 1566, at Gray's Inn in London, George Gascoigne and

Francis Kinwelmarsh produced an English version of Dolce's *Giocasta*, which, at a third remove from the original, they were able to pass off as translated directly from Euripides.[9]

As a kind of climax of sixteenth-century interest in Sophocles' tragedy, one can point to the decision, after long deliberation, of those who called themselves the Accademia Olimpica ("Olympian Academy") in Vicenza, to open its new theater, designed by Palladio, a fellow-member of the Academy, with a performance of *Oedipus the King* in Italian translation (1585). The translator, Orsato Giustiniani, adhered to the original as closely as possible, while the scenographer indulged his imagination. When the curtain was raised, the audience smelled incense, which the Thebans were burning to placate the gods (an idea prompted by line 4 in Sophocles). Oedipus, dressed like the Sultan of Turkey, appeared with a guard of twenty-four archers and surrounded by pages and eminent persons. Jocasta was accompanied by pages and ladies of honor. Creon, too, had his suite. The music of the chorus was composed by the contemporary Andrea Gabriele, the ancient music being lost. The actors did not wear masks, as did actors on the ancient stage.[10] The performance at Vicenza, then, starting from a translation of the ancient text, and with the goal of emulating an ancient performance, modernized the play in various respects. This tendency, no doubt inevitable, breaks down the opposition, proposed above, between the impulse to historical veracity and the impulse to adaptation. Even within the former, within the desire to honor the ancient work, as a sign, in the case of the Olympian Academy, of their classical ideals, a movement toward the present will occur.

OEDIPUS IN GERMANY

It would be a vast undertaking to trace the fortunes of the ancient and medieval Oedipus through all of Europe in the sixteenth century. For present purposes, two examples will show how differently, in this same period, Theban myth could be interpreted in the Protestant north. Philipp Melanchthon (1497–1560), friend and supporter of Luther, in his *Declamationes* emphasized the need to study classical Greek in order to understand the New Testament. He was professor of

Greek at Wittenberg, where he lectured on a few classical Greek texts, including Sophocles' *Antigone*, but not *Oedipus the King*. Something is known, from a surviving letter, of what he had to say about Euripides' *Phoenician Women*. On May 28, 1537, he wrote, in Latin:

> Tomorrow, God willing, at the sixth hour I shall begin an explication of Euripides' tragedy to which he gave the title *Phoenician Women*, in which he describes the two brothers fighting over the kingship, of Thebes, to both of whom ambition brought death. Discord arising hence generally overturns all empires, as Claudian said. For self-indulgence [*luxuria*] with its vices, and pride [*superbia*] with its hatreds, overturn the others. Of this fact this tragedy provides a shining example. It contains great speeches, by which it exhorts to restraint [*modestia*], and it teaches that we should take thought for the common safety of the citizens and not lead the state into danger, driven by desire [*cupiditas*], pride [*gloria*], or other private passions. Grasp of these precepts is useful for character, especially in these wretched times. Therefore I exhort the students to listen to this tragedy.[11]

Melanchthon has not abandoned a political reading of the tragedy, but he diagnoses the conflict between the brothers in a Christian vocabulary of personal virtues and vices.

Hans Sachs (1494–1576) was a shoemaker in the city of Nüremberg and, like Melanchthon, a Reformer. He was one of those tradesmen who had a parallel career as poet and singer, having emerged from his local singing school as a Meistersinger or master singer. He provides the character of the Meistersinger in Richard Wagner's opera of this name (1868). Sachs used the story of Jocasta in three works, a song of sixty lines, "Queen Jocasta" (1537), a play, *A tragedy, to be recited with thirteen persons, the unhappy queen Jocasta* (1550), and an aphoristic poem, "Story: the unhappy queen Jocasta" (1563). The narrative model for each of these works is Boccaccio's *De claris mulieribus/On famous women*.[12]

As a dramatization of Boccaccio's narrative, without reference to (and perhaps without knowledge of) either Sophocles' or Seneca's Oedipus tragedy, Sachs' is a new play. It includes scenes in Corinth; the leave-taking of Jocasta by Laius when he goes to fight for the Phoenicians (sic) against the Corinthians; the knightly meeting of Laius and Oedipus on the battlefield; a letter from the king of Corinth to Jocasta proposing that she marry his foster-son, and her letter in reply. Oedipus prospers as king of Thebes but is pained that he does not know who his parents are. Jupiter sends Mercury to tell Jocasta that Oedipus is her son, the one whom Laius intended to destroy. A jewel given to Oedipus when he was born, still in his possession, confirms the revelation. He blinds himself and goes into exile. The fifth and final act of the play concerns the sons of Oedipus and Jocasta, who are called Floristes and Joristes. They begin to quarrel. Jocasta tells them that she will continue as regent until they are older and can agree on how to share power. At this point, "Satan the sycophant" warns Joristes that he is being deceived by his brother, whom the queen in fact supports. Joristes and Floristes then fight a duel and kill each other. Jocasta stabs herself and dies. The herald speaks the epilogue, in which he draws five lessons from the tragedy. First, what God has decided must come to pass in its time. Second, happiness is transitory. Third, as for him who has been afflicted by unhappiness, "The cross is a medicine for the soul." He should not lay his own hand to himself. He should bear his cross. Fourth, everyone should be content with the power and wealth which God has given him. Fifth, regents should not give ear to wheedling courtiers.

Luther's teachings inspired a whole devil literature in the sixteenth century, and the appearance of Satan (in the form of a sycophantic courtier) in Sachs' play is almost predictable.[13] From the ancient Erinys or the curse of Oedipus as the cause of the conflict between the brothers, one has now arrived at Satan. The lesson Satan provides (number five) happens to be a secular one. The Christian recasting of the story comes out especially in the third message. Whereas the medieval Christian form of the story provided for the repentance of Oedipus, the shorter form in Sachs (Oedipus' ultimate fate is left uncertain) allows the poet to moralize the self-blinding. It is an example of a failure to bear one's cross.

THE SEVENTEENTH CENTURY: OEDIPUS IN FRANCE

At the beginning of the seventeenth century, the locus of Theban tragedy shifts to France. A last (Senecan) *Oedipus* remains to be written in Italy, that of Emanuele Tesauro (1661). In France, a series of Oedipus tragedies, which can be interpreted as a series of responses to the actual and the ideological turmoil of the French monarchy, begins with the performance of Jean Prévost's Senecan *Oedipus* in 1605. As king and father, Oedipus crystallizes the problems of family, state, religion, and law which present themselves to the Ancien Régime. A few years after the publication of Prévost's tragedy, Tallement des Réaux follows with another (Sophoclean) *Oedipus* (1614). Jean de Rotrou presents his *Antigone* in 1638. With the monarchy re-established after the Fronde or revolutionary period of mid-century, Pierre Corneille in his *Oedipus* (1659), as will be seen, shows a path to royal legitimacy. Jean Racine presented *La Thébaïde* in 1664, a surprisingly bleak culmination of seventeenth-century Theban drama – an example of what George Steiner has called "absolute tragedy."[14] The tragedies just named begin a tradition of Oedipus in French drama which has continued up to the present.[15] For this tradition, Corneille's tragedy is foundational.

Corneille's Oedipus

Corneille makes two prefatory statements, an "Au Lecteur"/"To the Reader" and an "Examen"/"Examination," in both of which he gives the same list of his divergences from Sophocles. For the ladies in the audience, he refrains from bringing the blinded Oedipus on stage, and he adds the "happy episode" of Dirce and Theseus. She is the daughter of Laius and Jocasta, thus the step-daughter of Oedipus. Theseus is the king of Athens, present in Thebes, in love with Dirce, whom he wishes to marry. Oedipus opposes the marriage for reasons of state: it would create a powerful rival within Thebes. Obliged to go to Corinth, to the bedside of Polybus, who he believes is his father, he prefers to leave the kingdom in the hands of a less powerful son-in-law, Haemon (in other Theban tragedies the son of Creon, but Creon is not mentioned by Corneille). The importance of the "happy episode" both for this play and for the subsequent history of Oedipus drama cannot be overestimated. It replaces Sophocles' opening, in which the priest, the oracle from Delphi, and then Teiresias, establish the gods and the city, the divine and the human, as the "vertical" structuring terms of the action. In Corneille, Dirce as a legitimate pretender to the throne of Thebes, and the politics surrounding her, create a "horizontal" human structure.[16]

Because of the plague, Oedipus consults the oracle at Delphi; the response is unclear. He orders that the ghost of Laius be questioned, and he learns that a propitiatory victim of the blood of Laius is required. Dirce offers herself. Theseus wants to die in her place but is rebuffed by Jocasta. Putting together the oracle received by Laius with what Teiresias has learned from the ghost of Laius, she maintains that it must be Laius' son who killed him. Everything now depends on the testimony of Phorbas, who has been summoned. Oedipus recognizes him (not vice versa) as one of those at the crossroads, and now realizes that he himself killed Laius. He does not yet know that he is Laius' son. Theseus, who has earlier been led by Phorbas' daughter (the maid of Dirce!) to believe that he is Laius' son, challenges Oedipus to a duel, to avenge his supposed father, Laius. Then a messenger comes from Corinth, and the discovery proceeds much as in Sophocles. The end of Jocasta, however, comes when Phorbas stabs her and she then also stabs herself.

Corneille says that he cut down the number of oracles, which would have made it all too easy for Oedipus to recognize his identity. (The courtier Dymas brings the oracle from Delphi. It is unclear, and unlike the Sophoclean one, determines nothing. In fact, it is Jocasta who suggests that the gods are angry because of the murder of Laius. What comes from Delphi in Sophocles comes from a human being in Corneille.) Corneille made the response of Laius evoked by Teiresias (here at least Corneille follows Seneca) obscure enough to be wrongly applied to another character, namely, Dirce. He sought reasons to justify what Aristotle found without reason, in particular the fact that Oedipus did not know the manner of Laius' death (*Poetics* 1460a27–31). Corneille's Oedipus in fact remembers that he killed two robbers, but he believes that, in doing so, he might actually have been killing the ones who killed Laius.[17]

In discovering his identity, Corneille's Oedipus only learns that he has committed the crimes of parricide and incest. Unlike Sophocles', he does not at the same time have to suffer the realization that he has fulfilled the prophecies received by his parents and by him. Corneille's can see himself as the completely innocent victim of the gods:

> My memory is full of nothing but noble deeds.
> Yet I find myself incestuous and a parricide,
> though I trod not but in the steps of Alcides [Heracles],
> nor sought I everywhere but for laws to maintain,
> for monsters to destroy and for wicked ones to punish.
> In spite of myself, heaven's order binds me to crimes.
> To make me fall into them, it hides me from myself.
> It offers, blinding me to that which it has predicted,
> my father to my sword, my mother to my bed.
> Alas, how true that we vainly imagine
> we can hide our life from heaven's destiny!
> Our exertions to escape make us run to meet it
> and our skill at flight plunges us the sooner therein.
> But if the gods have made my life abominable,
> they have through pity made its outcome honorable,
> since in the end their favor mingled with their anger
> condemns me to die for the salvation of all,
> and since, at the same time that my life must
> bear the ignominy of the crimes that they have caused me,
> the luster of those virtues, which I do not have from them,
> receives in recompense a glorious death. (1820–40)

Oedipus, in accordance with the response of Teiresias, which called for the expiation of Laius' murder with blood, anticipates his death. Though he refers to human attempts to escape "heaven's destiny," he himself never made such an attempt, for the simple reason that, absent the oracles, he had no reason to do so. His misfortune therefore presents itself to him as an incursion from a separate, hostile order which he can still resist. His virtues, he says, were won independently of the gods, and his death, even if ordained by the gods, is honorable.

As soon as the blood from Oedipus' eye sockets hits the ground, two sick persons in the court are healed, a sure indication that Oedipus' sacrifice will save the state. Acceding to the demand of Laius, as conveyed by Teiresias, Oedipus regains divine sanction, while Theseus, with his fine human qualities, assumes the royal power. Corneille thus offers, at the end, a complex but hopeful picture of royal power, a legitimization in advance of some future good king, perhaps a Louis XIV.[18] Though every explicit statement in the play concerning monarchy is loyalist, a hostile contemporary critic could find an anti-monarchist tendency in the very subject matter. The Abbé d'Aubignac, in a diatribe against Corneille's *Oedipus* published in 1663, wrote:

> Corneille should remember that he is putting his *Oedipus* on the French stage, which is not the place where one should exhibit the great misfortunes of royal families, when they are mingled with detestable and shameful actions and the subjects find themselves enveloped in the punishments for them which Heaven imposes on earth. What is the good of making people see that these crowned heads are not protected from ill fortune, that the disorders of their lives, though innocent, are exposed to the rigor of superior powers . . .?[19]

The Abbé's criticisms are of no interest in themselves; they show how anti-royalist implications could be perceived by a (perhaps willfully) simpleminded critic.

The *Oedipus* of John Dryden and Nathaniel Lee

Corneille's *Oedipus* soon found imitators in England. The *Oedipus* of John Dryden and Nathaniel Lee (fall 1678) prompts a detour into English literature or, more precisely, Restoration tragedy.[20] In their preface, the English dramatists are dismissive of Seneca and Corneille: "All that we could gather out of Corneille was, that an episode [i.e., the "happy episode"] must be, but not his way; and Seneca supplied us with no new hint, but only a relation which he makes of his Teiresias raising the ghost of Laius: which is here performed in view of the audience. . . ."[21] Dryden and Lee's subplot, concerning Creon, Eurydice, daughter of Laius, and Adrastus, her lover, is certainly not happy, as will be seen, but it follows Corneille's in providing political intrigue. Dryden and Lee fill their tragedy with favorite Elizabethan and Jacobean effects – a malevolent hunchback (Creon), a sleepwalking scene, the necromancy just mentioned, dreams, apparitions in the sky, repeated appearances of a ghost (Laius'), scheming courtiers, and a bloodbath at the end. The following summary attempts to isolate the main action.

As the play opens, the plague is raging in Thebes. Oedipus is away, fighting against the Argives. Creon is in love with Eurydice, who despises him. She is in love with the Argive Adrastus, who was earlier in Thebes as a hostage. Teiresias forestalls a popular uprising against Oedipus. The king returns with Adrastus his prisoner, whom he releases to go to Eurydice. The people, through their priests, supplicate Oedipus. Dymas, who had been sent to Delphi for an oracle concerning the plague, has just returned, and he quotes the oracle. Oedipus curses the murderer of Laius, as in Sophocles. Jocasta appears, and asks that Oedipus marry Eurydice to Creon. Oedipus refuses, on the grounds that it would be incestuous.

In the second Act, Oedipus summons Teiresias, who says that "the first of Laius' blood his life did seize" (2.1.173). Creon accuses Eurydice, the daughter of Laius. Adrastus, her lover, draws his sword and wounds Creon. Creon then accuses Adrastus of having murdered Laius because Laius refused him as a son-in-law. Oedipus calls on Teiresias for instruction. Creon's malice continues. He longs to possess Eurydice and the throne. In the first scene of the third Act, Creon's aspirations and Eurydice's loathing of him are reiterated. Adrastus falsely admits to the murder of Laius, in order to die in place of Eurydice, who is still under suspicion. Creon taunts Adrastus, who draws his sword. Haemon intervenes. Teiresias performs the necromancy. The ghost of Laius names Oedipus as his murderer, and Oedipus questions Teiresias on his findings.

The action now follows Sophocles' tragedy, except that Creon pretends to support Oedipus, telling him that Eurydice and Adrastus have suborned Teiresias. Jocasta's reassurance of her husband causes her, as in Sophocles, to refer to the murder of Laius in a way which makes Oedipus begin to suspect himself. He sends for the sole survivor of the affray at the crossroads, called Phorbas, as in Seneca. In Act 4, Creon stirs up the people against Oedipus, but the king calms them. An ambassador arrives from Corinth to report the death of Polybus. The revelation proceeds as in Sophocles. Oedipus is about to kill himself; Adrastus kicks the sword away. Teiresias says that Oedipus may reign in Corinth. As Act 5 opens, Creon believes that Thebes is now his. Haemon brings a report of the self-blinding of Oedipus, who now appears with Jocasta. They reaffirm their continuing love for each other. The ghost of Laius interrupts them. Haemon confines Oedipus in a tower to protect him from Creon, who has taken Eurydice prisoner. The play ends with a bloodbath. Creon kills Eurydice. Adrastus kills Creon. Creon's men kill Adrastus. A messenger reports that Jocasta has hanged herself, having first hanged her daughters and stabbed her sons to death. Oedipus appears in the window of his tower, makes his last speech, and jumps.

The play ends with Thebes, as far as its government is concerned, a tabula rasa. If anyone's policies or views are left intact, they are those of Teiresias, a reasonable and cautious priest, despite his obligatory incantations and other reflexes of the Greek and Latin models. The Theban people are a fickle and unruly mob. Creon could in fact have been a legitimate claimant to the throne. His complete lack of scruple disqualifies him morally; his death frees Thebes from his taint. Oedipus displays every virtue in this play. He would have been the lineal successor of the king of Thebes. He has every qualification for the kingship and, hypothetically, full legitimacy; at the same time, he has rendered himself illegitimate and worse. He kills himself. Dryden and Lee seem to offer no answer to the political question.[22]

Voltaire's *Oedipus*

In the seventeenth century and on through the eighteenth, France was the home of Oedipus. With Corneille's *Oedipus*, Sophocles displaces Seneca, and, although the Roman tragedian is never completely forgotten, a specifically Sophoclean tradition begins. André Dacier's preface to his translation of Sophocles' *Oedipus the King* confirms the tendency (1692). When Voltaire defends his *Oedipus* (1719, the year after the first performances), he does so with reference to Sophocles, to Corneille, and to Dacier's preface. By 1781, Oedipus' tragedy has become a chapter in the history of French literature. The Count of Lauraguais publishes his *Dissertation on the Oedipuses*, covering the tragedians just named, some lesser lights, and also his own *Jocasta* (also 1781). If the posthumous publication of Marie-Joseph Chénier's *Oedipus the King* in 1818 is taken as the end of the period, France saw seventeen adaptations of Sophocles' tragedy (including two parodies and two operas) in the eighteenth century. Of these, Voltaire's was the most successful in its own time. It was translated into English by Tobias Smollett.[23] It is the only one, besides Corneille's, still read.[24]

The play begins with the arrival of Philoctetes in Thebes. He has come to bury the ashes of Heracles, the companion of Philoctetes' later years. Philoctetes was once in love with Jocasta, whose father forced her to marry Oedipus. A plague afflicts Thebes. The High Priest has seen and heard the ghost of Laius, who was murdered four years earlier: Laius' murderer is in Thebes and must be punished. Oedipus, king now for two years, undertakes an investigation. Jocasta tells him that Phorbas, to whom Laius had given "half his power," brought the corpse back to Thebes and reported "villains unknown" (plural). The people suspected Phorbas, and Jocasta sent him to a "neighboring castle."

Act 2 focuses on Philoctetes. The people now suspect him of having murdered Laius. Jocasta, who still loves Philoctetes, is distraught. They meet and Jocasta urges him to leave Thebes. Oedipus enters, and asks Philoctetes to defend himself. The issue is left unresolved. Oedipus reveals to Araspes, his confidant, that he was ashamed to accuse Philoctetes. All his hopes, he says, rest on Phorbas, and he complains of his delay. The scene concludes with Oedipus and Araspes staking out positions on the degree of trust to be placed in priests and oracles. Act 3 opens with Jocasta's decision that Philoctetes must leave, no matter what suspicions concerning her may be aroused in the people. He refuses to leave because it would be taken as proof of his guilt. Oedipus promises to protect him from the people, though he himself has not decided whether Philoctetes is innocent or guilty. The issue between Philoctetes and Oedipus is dropped when the High Priest declares that Oedipus is the murderer. Philoctetes immediately displays his nobility by saying that he will not seek any advantage from the declaration. Oedipus turns on the priest, who replies with a prophecy of Oedipus' future wanderings and misery.

Oedipus is left with doubts. At the beginning of Act 4, he asks Jocasta to describe Laius. He concludes that he is the murderer and that the priest was right. As in Sophocles, Jocasta denounces prophecy. She tells the story of the oracle she received concerning her son and how she "sacrificed" him. (She does not describe an exposure.) Phorbas arrives and confirms that Oedipus is the murderer of Laius. Oedipus announces his departure from Thebes. Dymas arrives with the news that a messenger has come from Corinth. So ends Act 4. Oedipus prepares to leave Thebes. He recommends Philoctetes as king, and sends for Phorbas, whom he wants to reward. The Corinthian Icarus arrives with news of Polybus' death. Icarus warns him not to go to Corinth. The son-in-law of Polybus has succeeded him. Oedipus is indignant. To console him, Icarus explains that Oedipus was not in fact the son of Polybus. Icarus rescued him on Mt. Cithaeron, where "some kind god conducted him" (i.e., he was not a shepherd as in Sophocles). Phorbas arrives. From the encounter between him and Icarus the truth emerges. Oedipus reveals his identity to Jocasta. He blinds himself (offstage). Jocasta stabs herself. Oedipus does not appear in the final scene. Jocasta has the last words.

Jocasta was the first thing which Voltaire had to justify. The Letters which preface the publication of his tragedy begin with a defense against various calumnies which the author has suffered. One of them is that, because Jocasta scorns the oracles of Apollo, Voltaire "has no religion." Voltaire brushes aside the calumny (it is Jocasta, not I), but, on any reading of his tragedy, Jocasta, hardly the only critic of the gods, is, amongst the characters, their most outspoken critic. Both Philoctetes and, though more cautiously, Oedipus express the same views. Jocasta has the final words of the play, which can be compared with Oedipus' final words in Corneille, quoted above. To the High Priest she says that, because of the incest she has committed,

> Death is the only benefit, the only god which remains for me.
> Laius, receive my blood, I follow you among the dead.
> I have lived as a virtuous woman, and I die without regret.

And, after a one-line expression of sympathy from the chorus:

> Do not weep for my son, because he still breathes.
> Priests, and you Thebans, who were my subjects,

Honor my pyre, and bear in mind forever
That in the midst of the horrors of the destiny which oppresses me
I have made the gods blush who forced me to the crime.

Unlike Corneille's Oedipus, who still recognized "heaven's order," Jocasta defies the gods, who have shown themselves unjust. Voltaire's breezy self-justification, as regards her blatant impiety, in his Letters were not the final words to be spoken on this matter. Controversy followed, and the Jesuit Father Folard, at the behest of the archbishop of Lyon, in 1722 produced a new *Oedipus* to counter Voltaire's.[25]

The Letters on Sophocles and Corneille concern what might be called formal and aesthetic matters, though these, as will appear, are not unrelated to ideology. The Letter on Sophocles is the longest and the most outspoken. Applying the principle of probability or verisimilitude (*vraisemblance*), Voltaire finds a whole series of faults in Sophocles' tragedy. He is especially disturbed by Oedipus' numerous missed opportunities to get at the truth. "This Oedipus who explained the riddle does not understand the clearest things." Voltaire is somewhat more respectful of Corneille. "Corneille well knew that the simplicity or rather the dryness of Sophoclean tragedy could not furnish the full extent required by our theatrical pieces." Corneille thus added the episode of Theseus and Dirce. But Voltaire's approbation ends there, and his criticism starts at the same point. The character of Theseus is improbable. His passion "forms the whole subject of the tragedy and the misfortunes of Oedipus are only the episode" which Theseus was supposed to supply. Though there is no evidence that Voltaire knew Dryden and Lee's *Oedipus* or its preface, his criticism of Corneille is much like theirs. Ironically, his own subplot concerning Philoctetes and Jocasta becomes, like theirs, and like Corneille's in the first place, more important than the main plot. At the end of Voltaire's tragedy, who but the virtuous, enlightened Philoctetes is king? The subplot, which in his Letters Voltaire discusses in aesthetic terms, ultimately carries the ideological brunt.

DECLINE OF THE *POETICS*

To criticize Sophocles was to criticize Aristotle, whose authority, more than anything else, had made *Oedipus the King* the model for tragedy. Voltaire's iconoclasm reached its limit at this point. He refrained from mentioning Aristotle in his Letters. Dacier, a typical Aristotelian, made a good substitute, and it is Dacier whom he criticizes. But, with Voltaire, the authority of the *Poetics* for tragedy and for *Oedipus the King* in particular is in jeopardy. Toward the end of the century, it can be explicitly challenged. In 1781, a certain Gabriel Henri Gaillard wrote an essay on Aristotle and French classical drama from Corneille to his own time. The Aristotle who emerges from this essay is, in the words of Christian Biet, a "revised and corrected" one.[26] *Oedipus the King* will continue to determine the reception of the Oedipus myth in the nineteenth century, but now without Aristotelian constraints.

OVERVIEW

A new phase of Oedipus reception begins with the rediscovery of Sophocles in the fifteenth century. The success of *Oedipus the King* in the next century owes much to the authority of Aristotle, who, in his *Poetics*, took this tragedy as the example of the best plot-construction. At the same time, Seneca and Euripides remain influential, and a Giovanni Andrea dell' Anguillara melds parts of their Theban plays into a creative adaptation of *Oedipus the King* (1560). The new Greek texts spread quickly throughout Europe. Melanchthon is lecturing on Euripides' *Phoenician Women* in Wittenberg already in 1537, pointing out Christian virtues and vices in this tragedy. In the seventeenth century, France succeeds Italy as the center of Oedipus drama. Corneille's *Oedipus* is pivotal. Sophocles now eclipses Seneca as the model; a subplot becomes obligatory; Aristotelian authority weakens. Dryden and Lee in their *Oedipus* follow suit. The tendencies seen in Corneille culminate in Voltaire's *Oedipus* and in the Letters which he wrote to justify his tragedy. For the first time, critical detachment from the Sophoclean model, and, by clear implication, from Aristotle, can be definitively asserted.

5

THE INWARD TURN: NINETEENTH AND TWENTIETH CENTURIES

In the modern period, work on myth divides, in the case of Oedipus, into three kinds. First, imaginative work continues in translations and dramatic adaptations, opera, painting, and in the new media of film and modern dance. Second, philosophy, and later anthropology and psychology, analyze the Oedipus myth, and Oedipus attains a conceptual status. Third, in the new academic disciplines which take shape in the nineteenth century, the ancient Greek Oedipus tragedies and those of the national literatures become the object of literary-historical and literary-critical study. This third kind of work had begun already with humanist scholars in the fifteenth and sixteenth centuries. These three kinds of work on the Oedipus myth often intersect. The material which a history of the Oedipus myth has to consider is even vaster than in the earlier periods, and discussion accordingly becomes even more selective, guided by acknowledged high points and, inevitably, by individual preferences.

HÖLDERLIN AND HEGEL

Discussion of Oedipus in the Romantic period (1775–1830) amounts to a roll call of great names.[1] Amongst them, Friedrich Hegel (1770–1831) and Friedrich Hölderlin (1770–1843) stand out. The latter, the friend of Hegel, perhaps the author of the "Oldest System-Program of German Idealism," translated *Oedipus the King* and also published notes on his translation (1804). He meditates on Oedipus in the last section of the prose-poem "In Lovely Blueness . . ." (1823).[2] In the notes to the translation, Hölderlin keeps the opposition of divine and human, as in Sophocles, but the divine is for him paraphrasable as "the power of nature." Oedipus' "wondrous, angry curiosity" drives him to break down the barrier between the human and this other realm.[3] Silent on the Sphinx and the riddle-solving, Hölderlin proceeds from an explication of Oedipus' reaction to the Delphic oracle at the beginning of the play (cf. p. 49). Oedipus' self-discovery is not simply the ascertainment of particular transgressions but moreover a kind of invasion into a forbidden knowledge. In Hölderlin's Oedipus, one sees the precursor of Friedrich Nietzsche's, who is distinguished by "arrogant knowledge."[4]

But Hegel's Oedipus owes nothing to Hölderlin's. Hegel took Oedipus to mark, in the history of the human spirit (or mind), a decisive moment. The Greeks free themselves from the Egyptian entrapment of the spiritual in the natural or material. For the Egyptians, the Sphinx is nothing but an enigma, an artistic shape forcing its way out of the animal form. "It is the Greeks who make the transition from this enigma to the clear consciousness of spirit [the word here translated "spirit" is often translated "mind"]; and they express it in the most naïve form in the story of the Sphinx, whose riddle was solved by the Greek Oedipus when he pronounced the answer to be: man" (from "Lectures on the Philosophy of Religion," 1831). Or "the content (of the riddle) is the human being, the free self-knowing spirit" [or "mind"].[5] In the *Lectures on Fine Art* (given 1823–29 and published posthumously in 1835), Hegel spoke of the Sphinx as "the symbol of the symbolic itself," meaning by the symbolic the stage in the history of art in which content struggles with form to express itself.[6] For Hegel, the Egyptian Sphinx epitomized this struggle, and he saw in the riddle an articulation of the human trying to free itself from the animal. Oedipus solves the riddle by answering, "Man," thereby bringing the content of the symbol to light. With this new interpretation, the Sphinx and the riddle-solving acquire a central importance in the Oedipus myth which they retain up to the present.

Hegel was not the first to take the riddle-solving as a key to the myth. August Wilhelm Schlegel in a lecture on Sophocles from the years 1809–11, after expressing certain misgivings about Sophocles' tragedy, states: "But that which gives so grand and terrible a character to this drama, is the circumstance which . . . is for the most part overlooked; that to the very Oedipus who solved the riddle of the Sphinx relating to human life, his own life should remain so long an inextricable riddle. . . ."[7] At the time of Schlegel's lectures, Jean-Auguste-Dominique Ingres was returning, though in a revolutionary mood, to the Oedipus of the ancient vase painters, Oedipus vis-à-vis the Sphinx. In 1808, he painted *Oedipus and the Sphinx*, the first of three versions and the first of a series of artistic representations of the scene which extends up to the present (fig. 9, see p. 108).

August von Platen makes fun of the humanistic interpretation of the Sphinx episode in *The Romantic Oedipus* (1829).[8] The play emerges from contemporary literary controversies, and satirizes amongst others a certain Karl Leberecht Immermann, who appears as Nimmermann. This character, who proposes to write a "Romantic Oedipus," holds a dialogue with the personified "Public," who agrees with him on the failings of Sophocles' *Oedipus*. Of these the worst is the Sphinx. The answer to the Sphinx's riddle is "man," while Sophocles, says Nimmermann, shows Oedipus on two feet and then, with a cane, on three, after he has blinded himself, but never on four. Thus Oedipus does not sufficiently qualify as the humanist hero of the Romantics. Nimmermann proposes to remedy this defect in his improved Oedipus tragedy by completing what Hegel once referred to as Oedipus' "solution of the riddle in his own person."[9]

To return to Hegel, for him the Greeks have not yet attained the full self-consciousness of the human spirit. In his *Lectures on Fine Art*, discussing *Oedipus the King* against the background of Antigone, for him the consummate tragedy and indeed the consummate work of art, Hegel says:

> What is at issue here is the right of the wide awake consciousness, the justification of what the man has self-consciously willed and knowingly done, as contrasted with what he was fated by the gods to do and actually did unconsciously and without having willed it. Oedipus has killed his father; he has married his mother and begotten children in an incestuous alliance; and yet he has been involved in these most evil crimes without either knowing or willing them. The right of our deeper consciousness today would consist in recognizing that since he had

neither intended nor known these crimes himself, they were not to be regarded as his own deeds. But the Greek, with his plasticity of consciousness, takes responsibility for what he has done as an individual and does not cut his purely subjective self-consciousness apart from what is objectively the case.[10]

While *Antigone* represents the perfect conflict or "collision" (between polis and family), the conflict in *Oedipus the King* takes place within Oedipus and produces a qualified form of consciousness still tied to "what is objectively the case." Hegel's thought here would have to be pursued in its own dimension of the progress of the human spirit (or mind) toward absolute freedom. For present purposes, the new stage Hegel marks in the reception of the Oedipus myth is what has to be defined. The old oppositions between human and divine intelligence, between freedom and necessity, and between guilt and redemption, are now abandoned, and the tragedy is set free for new possibilities of significance.

"Subjectivity" is one of the most difficult concepts in Hegel's philosophy. It is a term which cannot, however, be avoided if one wants to understand the new path on which Hegel put the history of Oedipus reception. What it does not mean is easier to say than what it does mean. It does not mean "personal" or "relative to each person," as opposed to "objectively true," nor does it mean "illusory" as opposed to "real." The basic element in Hegel's concept of subjectivity is the priority of the mind to any experience of the world. The history of the mind is its discovery of this status and the freedom which comes with this discovery. Philosophers are not at ease with Hegel's answers, or lack of answers, to the questions which surround this position. For present purposes, it is enough to see why Hegel found the central meaning of the Oedipus myth in the solving of the Sphinx's riddle, which was "the transition . . . to the clear consciousness of spirit (or mind)."

Hegel also lectured on *Oedipus at Colonus*. His enthusiasm for this tragedy, like his interpretation of the riddle-solving, must be seen against the background of a trend. Already in the eighteenth century, Sophocles' second Oedipus tragedy was a favorite subject for composers of opera and for painters. The most successful was Sacchini, whose *Oedipe à Colone*, which opened at Versailles in 1786, had 583 performances. Hegel saw one of them in Paris in 1828. The best-known musical work inspired by this tragedy, Felix Mendelsohn's, appeared somewhat later, in 1845.[11] In France, Jean-François Ducis' play *Oedipe chez Admète* (1778), revised as *Oedipe à Colone* (1797), inspired a series of paintings, which reflect the conditions of the period of the French Revolution (1789–1815). Two scenes, repeated again and again, expressed the plight and aspirations of returning émigrés: the pathetic exiles Antigone and Oedipus approaching Colonus or Antigone's intercession with her father on behalf of Polynices, whom, in Dacis' version, Oedipus forgives. The history of these paintings can be plotted on the larger history of post-Revolutionary France.[12]

Hegel's comments on *Oedipus at Colonus* follow from his notion of the newly won subjectivity of Oedipus. He speaks of "an inner reconciliation," which, because of its subjective character, already borders on the modern. He regards Oedipus as transfigured in death, and, in keeping with the modernity of his Oedipus, makes the striking comment: "This transfiguration in death is *for us*, as for him, a visible reconciliation within his own self and personality."[13] It would be only a short step to a Christian interpretation, and in his "Lectures on the Philosophy of Religion" of 1824, referring to the voice which calls to Oedipus at the end of Sophocles' tragedy, Hegel says, "This sounds more like a pure reconciliation of spirit, like a reception into grace so to speak, as in the Christian religion." In one of the versions of this lecture, however, Hegel withdraws the suggestion, and a few years later, in the *Lectures on Fine Art*, he explicitly denies a Christian reading in terms of sin, pardon, and eternal bliss.[14] Hegel's denial proves to be binding, with few exceptions, on future interpretation.

Nietzsche's Oedipus brings together the importance of the Sphinx in Hegel and Hölderlin's notion of forbidden knowledge. Nietzsche writes in *The Birth of Tragedy* (written 1871):

> Oedipus the murderer of his father, the husband of his mother, Oedipus the solver of the riddle of the Sphinx! What does the secret trinity of these fateful deeds tell us? There is a very ancient, popular belief, particularly prevalent in Persia, according to which a wise magus can only be born from incest: which we, with respect to the riddle-solving and mother-marrying Oedipus must immediately interpret as follows – that wherever prophetic and magic powers break the spell

of the present and future, the inflexible law of individuation . . . this must have been brought about by a monstrous transgression of nature – as in this instance incest, for how could nature be forced to give up its secrets otherwise than by a triumphant violation, that is, through the unnatural?[15]

Offering the image of a "triumphant" Oedipus, Nietzsche assigns a positive value to the hero's crimes (note that they form a "trinity" or triad with the riddle-solving), and in this way articulates his status as rebel. He had begun to acquire this status already several decades before *The Birth of Tragedy*.

WAGNER'S OEDIPUS

With Nietzsche, the nineteenth-century inward turn in the interpretation of the Oedipus myth is already complete. This turn meant above all a new emphasis on the Sphinx episode and a positive evaluation of Oedipus, despite his crimes. Nietzsche dedicated *The Birth of Tragedy* to Richard Wagner, in whose opera he saw "genuine musical tragedy" – the rebirth, in Germany, of Greek tragedy. Though in a second edition, fifteen years after the first, Nietzsche repudiated the new German music, i.e., Wagnerian opera, as nothing but romanticism, a link between Nietzsche and Wagner remains in their conceptions of Oedipus.[16] In 1868, shortly before the initial publication of *The Birth of Tragedy*, appeared the second edition of Wagner's massive *Opera and Drama*.[17] In this work, going back to 1852, Wagner laid the historical and theoretical foundations for the new kind of opera that was taking shape in *The Ring*. Wagner preferred the term "musical drama" or "drama," and he believed, as Nietzsche at first believed, that he was returning to Greek tragedy.

Wagner's chapter on Oedipus shows how he understood the nature of the German heroes whom he was putting on stage. He called this chapter: "The Legend of Oedipus: As Explanation of the Relation Between Individual and State."[18] Wagner saw in the individual, "free and determining himself out of his own being" (§261), the fountain which renews the state, while the state always tries to choke it. In order to present Oedipus as this kind of individual, he begins with the same observations which Hegel had made on the involuntary and unwitting nature of Oedipus' crimes, for which, nevertheless, Oedipus was willing to punish himself, taking society's point of view of the matter. At the same time, however, the very fact of these crimes proved, for Wagner, the force of human nature. They showed that the "instinctive individuality of human nature was possessed of a might, not only greater [than society's], but irresistible" (§242). Wagner turns from this observation immediately to the Sphinx, just as Nietzsche was to speak of parricide, incest, and riddle-solving as a "triad" of deeds. In the riddle-solving, Wagner sees a moment of triumph followed by the downfall, when Oedipus receives Jocasta as his reward for freeing Thebes from the Sphinx. Oedipus' victory over the Sphinx was only the prelude to a defeat. He therefore had ultimately to consider the riddle unanswered (§233). Wagner then says: "It is *we* [his emphasis] who have the first duty of solving that riddle; and to do that strictly by justifying individual instinct out of Society itself, as the latter's perpetually self-renewing life-giving and principal possession" (§244). The concept of Oedipus as embodying free individual instinct took a particular form in nineteenth-century painting, discernible already in Ingres' Oedipus painting of 1808.

THE SPHINX IN ART

In order to grasp this new concept in Ingres, one has first to put oneself in touch with the tradition from which he was departing. In the scores of ancient vase paintings concerning the Theban Sphinx, the painters limited themselves to two basic scenes: in one a group of Thebans try to solve the riddle of the Sphinx; in the other, it is Oedipus alone face to face with the Sphinx. In both of these scenes, the Sphinx is always central or prominent, and, taken together, they amount to a version of the myth: a riddling monster afflicts Thebes, carrying off its young men one by one, until Oedipus, a young man from another city, solves the riddle and thus destroys the monster. The fidelity of the Greek eye to this fundamental image of Oedipus is shown by the astonishing fact that there are only a few Greek vase paintings illustrating other episodes in his life.[19]

In *Oedipus and the Sphinx* Ingres produced a modern version of the second of these scenes and initiated a new series, in which painters like Max Ernst implicitly or explicitly acknowledge his precedence. In ancient vase paintings Oedipus typically wears traveler's garb. In Ingres, he is nude, with only a token cloak, which serves to accentuate his nudity. As a nude, this Oedipus simultaneously achieves two quite different goals: innovation as regards the iconographic tradition, and compliance with the requirement that, on scholarship at the French Academy in Rome, Ingres submit a study of a live studio model. Ingres' innovation extends to the painting of the Sphinx, in which her human breasts, the closeness of the two figures, and the gaze of Oedipus are highlighted. The gaze, which is directed at the breasts and seems to penetrate the Sphinx, has been taken to represent the vision of the artist.

If this interpretation is correct, then Ingres' painting is the first example of Oedipus as emblematic of the rebel, of the artist's break with the past. This is the Oedipus prefigured in Hegel's interpretation, first fully articulated in Wagner's, fulfilled in Nietzsche's, and to be encountered again and again in the nineteenth and twentieth centuries. The given exceptionality of Oedipus, the great transgressor, makes him the revolutionary subject matter par excellence, and he is thus the perfect means for the simultaneous assertion of the same stance of the new work of art vis-à-vis its tradition. Max Ernst's surrealist collage *Oedipus and the Sphinx* well illustrates this tendency. Ernst took a cut-out of Ingres' Oedipus, and hollowed out the chest, literally intervening in the foundational image of the modern iconographical tradition of Oedipus. He replaced the head with the head and breasts of a Sphinx (fig. 10).[20] A jackal's head sits on Oedipus' lap. This collage appeared in his collection *A l'interieur de la vue* (1931), and, tantamount to a manifesto, was reproduced on the cover of the Max Ernst issue of the magazine *Cahiers d'Art* (1937).

Ingres has also taken the first step toward the eroticized scene which the Symbolists will favor. An explicitly amorous Sphinx emerges in Gustave Moreau's painting *Oedipus and the Sphinx* of 1864 (the same year as Ingres' third version of the work discussed above). The Sphinx, with a Quattrocento face and breasts, clings to the partly draped hero, her hind claws on either side of his genitals. To digress

Figure 9 Jean-Auguste-Dominique Ingres, *Oedipus and the Sphinx*. The Walters Art Museum, Baltimore.

for a moment, a written description of Moreau's painting was to inspire Cavafy's poem, "Oedipus," which ends with the same thought that Wagner expressed – Oedipus' victorious riddle-solving is only temporary.[21] The next step in the eroticization of the Sphinx is her kiss, realized first in a sculpture by Ernest-Louis-Aquilas Christophe, *The*

Figure 10 Max Ernst, *Oedipus and the Sphinx*. Collage reproduced on cover of Max Ernst issue of *Cahiers d'Art* (1937).

Figure 11 Fernand Khnopff, *The Caresses* (1896). Royal Museums of Fine Arts, Brussels. Courtesy of the Royal Museums of Fine Arts of Belgium, Brussels.

Supreme Kiss (1891). In Franz von Stuck's painting *The Kiss of the Sphinx* (1895), the monster has the head and breasts of a woman, and, reaching down from her ledge, embraces and forcefully kisses the nude hero. Another Symbolist, the Belgian Fernand Khnopff, executed *The Caresses* in 1896 (fig. 11). Here the Sphinx is a cheetah with a woman's head. The pansy above the youth's ear is a signature which Khnopff used in other paintings, and here identifies the artist with Oedipus. (The painting had the alternate title *Art*.[22]) The painter identifies himself with his transgressive subject as he challenges the established iconography of the scene.

JOSÉPHIN PÉLADAN AND HUGO VON HOFMANNSTHAL

The Symbolist painters' Sphinx belongs to a broader fin de siècle conception of the femme fatale. The triumph of Oedipus is now his resistance to this dangerous woman, and it is even possible to rewrite the myth so that it ends with this triumph. Joséphin Péladan did so in his play *Oedipus and the Sphinx* (1897). In the first Act, Oedipus kills Laius. The scene is dramatized. In the second Act, Teiresias tells Jocasta that, if the Thebans renounce vengeance on the murderer, they will, by tomorrow, be rid of the Sphinx. The High Priest (a character distinct from Teiresias) decides that Jocasta will be the reward for the savior. She is indignant ("I should dedicate my bed, still warm from the dead man, to a new husband?") but decides to do it for the good of the city. Oedipus arrives. He reminds Jocasta of Laius and of an infant dead in the cradle. Oedipus departs to face the Sphinx. In the stage directions for Act 3, as if with the painters' Sphinx in mind, Péladan writes: "The Sphinx has the head and the thrusting nude breasts of a beautiful young woman; the paws and what can be seen of the body are a panther's." When her threats fail to turn the young hero aside, the Sphinx tries to seduce him:

> Give a kiss to the vermilion lip which begs you.
> Once you know the caress of the Sphinx
> all other pleasure will be impossible for you.
> In my embrace, you will believe that you possess the mystery.

An ineffable joy will heat your veins
and you will believe yourself god, under the power of pleasure.

Oedipus resists and the Sphinx disappears with a terrible cry. Oedipus then falls asleep in front of the Sphinx's cavern. During the night, the Thebans and Jocasta go out from the city carrying torches. Jocasta proclaims Oedipus savior of Thebes and her husband. Such is the triumphal ending of the play.[23]

Péladan's play is remembered today only as the inspiration for Hugo von Hofmannsthal's *Oedipus and the Sphinx* (1906). In broad outline, though with different characters and sometimes different action, the three acts of Hofmannsthal's play follow those of Péladan's. Hofmannsthal, however, intended something far more ambitious than his Parisian model. His play was to be the first part of a trilogy, to be followed by his translation of Sophocles' *Oedipus the King* (performed in 1910), and a third play, never written, corresponding to *Oedipus at Colonus*. In this way, Hofmannsthal would have given the two Sophoclean Oedipus tragedies a new context and a meaning. What this meaning would have been is intimated in the epigraph to *Oedipus and the Sphinx*, taken from Hölderlin's *Hyperion*: "The surge of the heart would never rise in such splendor and become spirit did not the reefs of fate stand mutely in its course."[24] "Spirit" is a key term in German idealism and in Hegel in particular. But in Hofmannsthal's plan the overcoming of the Sphinx does not, contrary to Hegel, stand for "spirit." On the contrary, the Sphinx is one of the reefs of fate. The Sphinx poses no riddle. She recognizes Oedipus and calls him by name before she, in effect, commits suicide. Oedipus perceives that his easy victory is really a defeat, trapping him in the chain of events predicted by the priestess at Delphi. Only in the third play, as Hugo von Hofmannsthal's surviving notes show, would the level of spirit be attained.[25]

As for "the surge of the heart," the phrase points to a central theme in the play, which is desire. Through the character of Creon, who aspires to the kingship of Thebes, Hofmannsthal distinguishes between ordinary human desire, on the one hand, and the kind of impersonal, sacral desire experienced by Oedipus, on the other. Communicating with his ancestors in the dreams which he has at

Delphi, Oedipus realizes that "[t]he flow of blood / is a dark, turgid flood into which the soul dives and finds no bottom." After he receives the prophecy, he understands why he has remained a virgin. He could only desire a queen. He could only beget children from a "sacred womb." Fatality in this play is the reflex of the royal bloodstream, which produces both the superhuman and the monstrous in the same person. Self-sacrifice, too, is entailed in the blood-driven career of this superior, Nietzschean (as commentators often point out) man. Already in the dreams at Delphi, Oedipus sees himself as "both the priest who swings the blade / and the sacrifice."[26]

SIGMUND FREUD

The Viennese Hofmannsthal shows no knowledge of the thought of his fellow-citizen Sigmund Freud (1856–1939), and his *Oedipus and the Sphinx* is the last creative work on the Oedipus myth which is not in the position of affirming or denying the new psychoanalytic interpretation. Freud articulates what he would later (in 1910) call the Oedipus Complex for the first time in a letter of October 15, 1897. "I have found love of the mother and jealousy of the father in my own case, too [i.e., as well as in his patients], and now believe it to be a general phenomenon of early childhood . . .," and he goes on to speak of Sophocles' *Oedipus the King* and also of *Hamlet*.[27] The first published statement of the Oedipus Complex comes in *The Interpretation of Dreams* (1900), one of only two extensive statements of the matter in all of Freud's many volumes. By this time, Freud has worked out the two ways in which he can use the Oedipus myth. First, it confirms the truth of the Complex. "This discovery [i.e., of the Oedipus Complex] is confirmed by a legend that has come down to us from classical antiquity." What Freud has in mind is the grip of Sophocles' tragedy on the audience, and it is in fact this one drama which for Freud constitutes the Oedipus myth. Second, the course of the discovery in Sophocles corresponds to the patient's self-discovery in psychoanalysis. In this respect, the incest dream to which Jocasta refers (lines 977–82: "Many men have slept with their mother in their dreams") is "the key to the tragedy." Indeed, Freud holds that the myth "sprang from some primeval [Oedipal] dream-material. . . ."[28] If so, then Freud has to explain where the dream came from, and his answer will be that it was an event in the earliest history of mankind, in fact, the foundational event of human history. To tell the story, he invents the myth of the primal horde, in *Totem and Taboo* (1913). The sons band together to kill the patriarch and get possession of his women. Having killed him, they are overcome by guilt, regulate their relations with the women, and now worship the dead patriarch in the form of their totem.

The influences in Freud's life which led him to the Oedipus Complex, the history of the psychoanalytic movement, feminist critique of Freud, the 1980s controversy over Freud's abandonment of real childhood trauma as the cause of neurosis, the Marxist "Anti-Oedipus" are quite beyond the scope of the present book.[29] In a history of the reception of the Oedipus myth, the question concerning Freud will be his relation to *Oedipus the King*, his sole source, to repeat, for the Oedipus myth. Though he certainly knew *Oedipus at Colonus*, he never mentions this tragedy.

It remains, then, to compare the Oedipus Complex and *Oedipus the King*, an easier task than one might have expected. The number of motifs which Freud takes over from the tragedy turns out to be surprisingly small. He does not discuss prophecy, exposure, or mutilation of the feet. The last of these motifs he could have interpreted in terms of the Castration Complex, the boy's fear of castration as punishment for his incestuous desires. If the Castration Complex supervenes upon and terminates the Oedipus Complex and "is of the profoundest importance in the formation alike of character and of neuroses," then it seems that Freud might have sought for a correspondence in the Oedipus myth.[30] He could have found it in the mutilation of Oedipus' feet, which he could have interpreted as a symbolic castration, over-determining the parents' attempt to prevent the prophesied incest by exposing their child. Nor does Freud have much to say about the self-blinding, except, in an allegorical vein, that "we live in ignorance of these wishes, repugnant to morality . . . and after their revelation we may all of us seek to close our eyes to the scenes of our childhood."[31] But the self-blinding too could have been interpreted as castration.[32]

Considering the nineteenth-century tradition of the Sphinx as a central episode in the Oedipus myth, a tradition of which Freud would have been at least partly aware, his neglect of the Sphinx is surprising. Though the Sphinx necessarily appears in his summary of the myth,[33] he does not integrate the monster-slaying into his interpretation. He several times refers to the riddle of the Sphinx as "the question of where babies come from," and this question, which initiates the "sexual researches" of children, is "in a distorted form which can easily be rectified . . . the same riddle that was propounded by the Theban Sphinx."[34] Freud seems to have a particular riddle in mind and to assume that his readers know it.[35]

Fate is now the Oedipus Complex. "It is the fate of all of us, perhaps, to direct our first sexual impulse toward our mother and our first hatred and our first murderous wish against our father."[36] Thus Freud in *The Interpretation of Dreams*. Twenty-six years later, in "The Question of Lay Analysis," he speaks more boldly. He holds a dialogue with an imaginary interlocutor called the "Impartial Person." Freud says to this Person: "I am surprised that you are still silent. That can scarcely mean consent. . . . In asserting that a child's first choice of an object is . . . an incestuous one, analysis no doubt once more hurt the most sacred feelings of humanity, and might well be prepared for a corresponding amount of disbelief, contradiction, and attack. And these it has received in good abundance. Nothing has damaged it more in the good opinion of its contemporaries than its hypothesis of the Oedipus complex as *a structure universally bound to human destiny*."[37]

Freud takes over the role of Apollo for himself, though with self-irony. In 1908, Freud supervised the treatment of a boy, not quite five years old, called Little Hans. On March 30, the boy and his father came to Freud's office and Freud reports the following concerning their session:

> I . . . disclosed to him [Little Hans] that he was afraid of his father, precisely because he was so fond of his mother. It must be, I told him, that he thought his father was angry with him on that account; but this was not so, his father was fond of him in spite of it, and he might admit everything to him without any fear. Long before he was in the world, I went on, I had known that a little Hans would come who would be so fond of his mother that he would be bound to feel afraid of his father because of it . . . 'Does the Professor [Freud] talk to God,' Hans asked his father on the way home, 'as he can tell all that beforehand?' I should be

extraordinarily proud of this recognition out of the mouth of a child, if I had not myself provoked it by my joking boastfulness.[38]

In sum, Freud drastically reduces the number of motifs in the Oedipus myth, effectively to two – parricide and incest; interprets them as standing for the desires of early childhood; and universalizes them. Oedipus the King is now everyman or everychild. With the Castration Complex, the superego comes into being, bringing a sense of guilt. A transfiguration of the hero, as in *Oedipus at Colonus*, is unthinkable in Freud's biological concept of man as a creature specifically defined by his instincts like other animals.

"AN OEDIPEMIC HAS BROKEN OUT"

The 1920s and 1930s saw the most intense work on the Oedipus myth in the whole history of its reception. Freud published *The Ego and the Id* (1923), "The Dissolution of the Oedipus Complex" (1924), *An Autobiographical Study* (1925), and "The Question of Lay Analysis" (1925–26), each with further reflections on the Oedipus Complex. Already in 1920, Freud's follower Theodor Reik extended the psycho-analytic interpretation of the Oedipus myth in his "Oedipus and the Sphinx," in which he argued that the Sphinx was a negative mother-figure. In the same year, Leoncavallo's opera *Edipo Re* premiered in Chicago. In 1922, George Enescu played a complete piano version of his opera *Oedipe*, which he had started in 1910, inspired by a performance of Sophocles' *Oedipus Rex* with the great actor Jean Mounet-Sully in the title role.[39] (He completed the orchestration in 1931.) Max Ernst's treatments of the Oedipus myth in various media begin with his painting *Oedipus Rex* in 1922, a surrealist manifesto. The Dadaists Francis Picabia and Salvador Dali explore the theme, the latter with explicit reference to Freud (1923 and 1930).

The time period in question offers longer lists of relevant names and titles, which do not have to be reproduced here.[40] The most interesting story, which includes the most significant works, concerns André Gide, Jean Cocteau, and Igor Stravinsky. The last named, in the pages of his autobiography for the year 1925, speaks of his desire to undertake "something big." "I had in mind an opera or an oratorio on some universally familiar subject." He asked Cocteau to be his librettist, and together they decided on Sophocles' *Oedipus the King* as the subject. Stravinsky sent back Cocteau's first drafts, wanting greater simplicity. From the first, he had intended Latin as the language of the libretto. He believed that Latin gave him "a medium not dead, but turned to stone and so monumentalized as to have become immune from all risk of vulgarization." Cocteau gave the French text of his libretto to a young Jesuit seminarian, Jean Daniélou, for translation. Stravinsky then proceeded to set the Latin to music but in defiance of Latin word accent.[41] Though Stravinsky continued in his old age to speak of Daniélou's Latin in glowing terms, it was not what he had hoped for. The libretto is a bizarre twentieth-century artifact of bastardized Latinity.[42] The music is another matter. Stravinsky's opera-oratorio *Oedipus Rex* (1927) is an acknowledged masterwork of twentieth-century music.

Cocteau's rejected first draft did not go to waste. He had in effect created a short play about Oedipus, which he read aloud in 1927; it was performed ten years later. It also formed the basis of the fourth act of his *The Infernal Machine* (1934). Gide began his *Oedipe* in 1930. Referring to Cocteau's play and the libretto for Stravinsky, Gide quipped "An Oedipemic has broken out."[43] Gide's play was first performed in 1932. The epidemic would include the now forgotten *Oedipus* of Claude Orly (1934), and perhaps some of the works listed at the beginning of this section. It continued with the premiere of Enescu's *Oedipe* in 1936 and, two years later, with the *Oedipus or The Twilight of the Gods* of Henri Ghéon.[44] The collaboration of Cocteau and Stravinsky resumed in 1952, when a full-scale production of *Oedipus Rex* took place in Paris and then toured elsewhere in Europe. Stravinsky agreed to a series of seven tableaux, with brief, mimed action, at intervals in the opera-oratorio: The Arrival, One Night, of the Plague at Athens (sic); Athene's Grief (Cocteau seems to confuse Thebes with Athens); The Oracles; The Sphinx; The Oedipus Complex; The Three Jocastas; and Oedipus and his Daughters.[45] Cocteau's backdrop, he says, was inspired by one of his drawings for *The Infernal Machine*, and much of the material in these tableaux is drawn from this play.

The tableau of the Oedipus Complex seems to go directly against the spirit of Stravinsky's opera-oratorio, one of the most un-Freudian of post-Freudian works on Oedipus. Stravinsky's conception appears to the present writer to be a fundamentally religious one (and, to take a biographical approach to the question, Stravinsky returned to the Russian Orthodox church in September 1925, the year in which he began to contemplate the idea of the big opera or oratorio). Stravinsky alludes musically to many operas, to the whole tradition of opera, as it were. But *Oedipus Rex* is operatic only in that it tells a story and characters enter and exit. The rather static oratorio form and the model of Handel in particular tend to dominate Stravinsky's composition and to suggest that a religious message is being conveyed.[46] Harmonic analysis shows an opposition between an E-flat "human-key" and a C-major "god-key." Recurring minor thirds signify fate, the fate which is going to teach Oedipus the Christian lesson of humility. Referring to the early days of their disagreements over the libretto, Cocteau remarks, "Stravinsky had Latinized himself to the point of willing a sort of Latin liturgy of the Greek drama."[47] Introducing a Speaker at various points, who fills in the narrative, Cocteau, for his part, attempted to preserve an ancient, pagan, or at least unspecific theology. The Speaker refers to "forces that watch us from a world beyond death." In the ancient tragedy, this is the world of the gods and is epitomized in Apollo, the god of prophecy. The music, however, of Stravinsky overwhelms the text of Cocteau, restating the ancient opposition between Oedipus and Apollo in Christian terms.

Stravinsky wrote the part of Oedipus as that of the operatic Heldentenor or hero tenor. In this way, the operatic movement within the oratorio structure can trace musically a movement from pride (the heroic Oedipus sees the plague as another chance for glory, like the Sphinx) to downfall. In *The Infernal Machine* a similar reduction of Oedipus to non-heroic human dimensions takes place, though within a different framework. On the one hand, the superhuman or divine realm consists simply of "infernal gods." The Voice at the beginning of the play says: "Spectator, this machine, you see here wound up to the full in such a way that the spring will slowly unwind the whole length of a human life, is one of the most perfect constructed by the infernal gods for the mathematical destruction of a mortal" (Sanderson and Zimmerman 1968: 182). On the other, the human actors, beginning with the frivolity of Jocasta and Teiresias, whom she calls "Zizi," are stripped of the high stature they have had in previous Oedipus drama. Characters make ironic, metatheatrical comments on the action: "a fine catastrophe," a "sordid drama," a "masterpiece of horror" (ibid.: 240, 242, 243). In fact, the given events of the myth or of previous Oedipus drama are what, in Cocteau's witty rendition, reduce Oedipus to the level of an ordinary man. At the end of the third Act, the Voice explains that the cruel gods make "of this playing-card king, in the end, a man" (ibid.: 237). The movement of the drama, then, is from the plane of decadent, smart set royalty to the plane of the people, to whom, Teiresias says, Oedipus now belongs (ibid.: 245).

Cocteau's most conspicuous means of achieving this end is what might be called the psychologizing, in Freudian hues, of the characters given in the myth. Though Jocasta complains of a recurring nightmare in which her nursling turns into paste and makes sexual advances toward her, she speaks approvingly of the union of mother and son.[48] Act 1, with the appearance of the ghost of Laius, invokes *Hamlet* and indirectly Freud, who both in the letter cited above and in his scientific writings, compared Hamlet to Oedipus. His early follower and his official biographer, Ernest Jones, published "Hamlet and Oedipus" in 1910, with a second, expanded version in 1923. Cocteau's second Act is entirely devoted to the encounter with the Sphinx, who is divided into two, a young woman, who falls in love with Oedipus and gives him the answer to the riddle, and her keeper, Anubis, who has a detachable jackal's head. This act reminds of the Sphinx-centered dramas of Péladan and Hofmannsthal, and the jackal's head might have been inspired by Ernst's collage. Again, as with the apparent allusion to Freud on Hamlet, Cocteau's relation to obvious precedents is unclear. The third Act is "The Wedding Night." As in Hofmannsthal, Oedipus is a virgin, though the point is now different. Oedipus says defiantly to Teiresias: "The high priest of a capital is astonished that a country boy should put all his pride in keeping himself pure for a single offering. You would, no doubt, have preferred a degenerate prince. . . ." So, curiously, it is qua man of the people that Oedipus had preserved his virginity. Jocasta dreams again of the paste. (One notices the straining for effect for which Cocteau was and is often blamed.)

Cocteau spoke of the fourth and final Act as "a sort of counter-action of the Greek drama."[49] Oedipus has escaped from the conditions of the ancient drama into modernity. Something similar happens in Gide's *Oedipus* though the terms of the escape are different. The play opens with Oedipus' saying: "Here I am, all present and complete in this instant of ever-lasting time, like someone who might come down to the front of the stage and say: I am Oedipus." From the outset, then, Gide drives a wedge between the ancient Oedipus (and, for that matter, the Oedipus of French drama), on the one hand, who is already complete and immortal as a character, and, on the other, the new Oedipus, the present speaker, who proceeds, in a rather arrogant self-description, to redescribe the other Oedipus. The chorus immediately objects to his "aggressive individualism." This individualism, which puts him in opposition to the priest Teiresias (who is "dressed as a friar") and the bourgeois Creon, is the mode of the new Oedipus' emergence from the tradition in which he came to Gide.

Oedipus states his credo in Act 2. His sons are reflecting on "the malady of the present age" (Eteocles has written a tract with this title), which they regard as inner doubt and questioning. The gods and monsters faced by earlier heroes and, for the last time, by their father, are now within us, says Eteocles. Oedipus, however, encourages his sons to believe that there are still monsters to be slain. Everyone faces a monster and a riddle. Though the riddle may differ, the answer is always the same: oneself. This principle of self remains intact in the face of the discovery of his identity. Resisting the recognition that the gods were in control of him all along (cf. in Sophocles "all this was Apollo"), this Oedipus seeks an escape: "I should like to invent some new form of unhappiness – some mad gesture to astonish you all, and astonish myself, and astonish the gods." He exits and blinds himself. Returning on stage, he debates with Teiresias; expresses indifference to the argument that the gods might also have foreseen his self-blinding; asserts it as an act of his own will. "I could go farther only by turning . . . against myself." He has already, at the time of the discovery, spoken of his crimes not as the fulfillment of his destiny but as holding him back, preventing him from fulfilling some unknown destiny which lies before him in the evening of his life.

VLADIMIR PROPP AND CLAUDE LÉVI-STRAUSS

As passages in his *Journal* show, Gide had little use for Freud, and the casual expression of incestuous desires by characters in his *Oedipus* can be taken as Gide's reaction to Freud's portentous pronouncements on the matter.[50] The major challenges to Freud's interpretation of the Oedipus myth had to come at the same level of conceptual work on the myth at which Freud himself was operating. The two most important came from a folklorist and an anthropologist specializing in mythology. The first of these, the great Russian folklorist and theoretician of narrative Vladimir Propp, published his essay on Oedipus folklore, "Oedipus in the Light of Folklore" in 1944. It did not become known in the West until an Italian translation in 1975, and was not translated into English until 1983.[51] Though Propp does not mention Freud in this essay, in aligning himself with the views of Frederick Engels, he puts himself on the side of those who were then stifling Freud's ideas in the Soviet Union. Propp seeks an explanation of the Oedipus myth in terms of its historical origin, which has left a palimpsest in folktales which have the same story pattern as the ancient myth. He uses these folktales comparatively in order to reach conclusions about the Oedipus myth. He finds that the evolution of human society from matrilineal to patrilineal forms of succession to power – he invokes Frazer's *The Golden Bough* as his authority for this history of kingship – has left a trace in these folktales. In the earlier matrilineal society, succession, conferred by a woman through marriage, is from the old king to a son-in-law. The successor kills the old king. In a more evolved stage of human history, succession is from father to son. The Oedipus myth transposes the conflict between old king and son-in-law into the conflict between Laius and his own son, which begins with the exposure of the newborn babe and ends with the murder of Laius. Propp's discovery of these traces of early human history in the Oedipus myth was written at a time when he had come under suspicion in the xenophobic and anti-Semitic atmosphere of the Soviet Union after World War II, and amounted to an avowal of solidarity with official Soviet doctrine, in particular Engels' *The Origin of the Family, Private Property, and the State*.[52] Engels had built his theory on the Frazerian evolutionary foundation which Propp reaffirms.

Although no one would now accept its main thesis on the Oedipus myth, Propp's essay remains fundamental for its analysis of individual motifs and for its demonstration of the unity of the two phases of the myth represented by Sophocles' two Oedipus tragedies. Freud's other main challenger was Claude Lévi-Strauss. His article, "The Structural Study of Myth" (1955), was a manifesto of his new structuralism. He chose two examples, one a Zuni Indian myth, the other the Oedipus myth. The structuralist interpretation of the latter aimed to replace the psychoanalytic one, though Lévi-Strauss referred to Freud only in passing. A fuller critique of Freud appeared in 1985 in *The Jealous Potter*, where Lévi-Strauss said that it was Freud's mistake in interpreting the Oedipus myth to privilege a single code, the sexual one, "while a myth will always put several codes in play."[53] Lévi-Strauss' interpretation of myths, especially those of the South American Indians in whom he specialized, brings out zoological, astronomical, culinary, and other codes as well as the sexual one, which, he maintains against Freud, is not even obligatory. It can be omitted. By implication, the importance of the sexual in human personality is vastly diminished.

Structuralist interpretation as set out in the article of 1955 rests on the linguistics of Ferdinand de Saussure and in particular on the distinction between *langue*, language as relatively unchanging system (of grammar, etc.), and *parole*, language as a stream of ever new events of speech. In myth, what corresponds to the second of these dimensions is the narrative, the sequence of events as they emerge in the story. The first, static dimension is, so to speak, invisible. It amounts to the structure of the myth, which the new method aims to reveal. Lévi-Strauss does not give rules for the analysis of structure but describes the empirical process by which he arrived at the structure of the Oedipus myth. He broke down the myth, which, for him, included the whole Labdacid myth and even the myth of the foundation of Thebes by Cadmus, into the shortest possible sentences, and wrote these on index cards. Then he shuffled the cards until patterns began to appear. For example, he found a group of cards showing motifs which he could label "over-rating of kinship relations," most notably Oedipus' incestuous marriage and Antigone's burial of Polynices. He found another group consisting of murders within the tribe or family

– the men who sprang from the dragon's teeth sown by Cadmus, the founder of Thebes, began to kill each other; Laius tried to kill Oedipus; Oedipus killed Laius; Eteocles and Polynices killed each other. Lévi-Strauss' rubric for this group was "under-rating of kinship relations." These two groups thus formed a binary opposition: over-rating vs. under-rating.

He found two more such groups, both having to do, this time, with autochthony, and again they stood in an oppositional relation, one affirming and the other denying the origin of humans from the earth. These two groups (C and D in fig. 12 below) revealed the underlying

	A	B	C	D
Bundles (read A–D vertically, but read A–C sequentially, left to right, for the story)	Oedipus marries mother Antigone buries brother	"Sown-men" kill each other Oedipus kills father Oedipus' sons kill each other	Cadmus kills dragon Oedipus kills Sphinx	Oedipus = "Swollen-foot"
Common feature of bundles (read A–D) vertically)	Over-rating of blood relations	Under-rating of blood relations	Denial of autochthony	Affirmation of autochthony
Logic		A: B :: C: D		

Figure 12 Lévi-Strauss' structural analysis of the Oedipus myth, with bundles selectively represented.

issue of the myth, which "has to do with the inability, for a culture [i.e., the ancient Greeks] which holds the belief that mankind is autochthonous . . . to find a satisfactory transition between this theory and the knowledge that humans are actually born from the union of man and woman."[54] The affirmation of autochthony (D) was, one might say, the most important bundle of motifs for Lévi-Strauss, and it was also the most problematical. He had to rely on the etymologies of the Labdacid names. Clearest was the name Oedipus (= "Swollen-foot"). This name, he said, indicates awkward walking, and this kind of walking is "a universal characteristic of men born from the earth." The etymologies of the other names remained speculative, as, many would say, was Lévi-Strauss' idea that the ancient Greeks were afflicted by the theory that men were once born from the earth.

He then saw that the two sets of binary oppositions stood in a proportional relation to each other: over-rating to under-rating as denial to affirmation. The myth is thus a logical tool which palliates the fundamental problem of autochthony by transposing it into terms of kinship relations. The most striking elements in the ancient myth, incest and parricide, become, in this structuralist approach, only elements of a code. They have no meaning in themselves, and a fortiori they do not have the meaning which Freud assigned them.

THE CHALLENGE OF THE SPHINX

Lévi-Strauss easily (whether or not correctly) disposed of the Sphinx in the interpretation of the myth just sketched. Her slaying by Oedipus was an example of the denial of autochthony. Lévi-Strauss had to face the Sphinx once again, however. With intellectual ambition even greater than he had shown the first time, he chose the Oedipus myth to illustrate the possibility of demonstrating "certain universal forms of thought." These forms would be concealed in mythical structures that necessarily differ from place to place and from one age to another. Lévi-Strauss' demonstration would be most effective if he could find a temporally and geographically distant myth which turned out to be the logical (i.e., not historical) transformation of the Oedipus myth. He found it in an Algonquin myth concerning brother–sister incest.

Because he considered the Sphinx episode integral to the Oedipus myth, he believed that he could clinch his argument for the American Indian myth as the logical equivalent of the ancient Greek one if he could show that the former included the Sphinx and her riddle. At the surface level, it includes neither. It does have, however, a woman, a powerful sorceress, the mistress of the owls, who learns from them the identity of the incestuous brother, the identical double of her own son. While there are other Algonquin myths in which owls set riddles for heroes to solve, in this myth the owls' role is to solve a "riddle," namely, the identity of the incestuous young man, whom the woman mistook for her own son. The only other example of riddles, almost non-existent in North American Indian cultures, which Lévi-Strauss could find came from the Pueblo Indians. Their ceremonial clowns, believed to be the offspring of incestuous unions, present riddles to their audiences. Putting these facts together, Lévi-Strauss concluded: "It follows that in America, also, riddles present a double Oedipal character, by way of incest on the one hand, and on the other hand, by way of the owl, in which we are led to see, in a transposed form, an American Sphinx." With "double Oedipal character," Lévi-Strauss seems to grant himself too much. Each of his two American Indian examples offers a more or less tenuous analogy to the Sphinx episode in the Oedipus myth. The combination of the two examples does little to make them relevant to the Algonquin myth, in which no riddle appears.[55]

The attempt of Lévi-Strauss to deal with the Sphinx is not reviewed here for its own sake, in order to make a critique of his thought, but as a glaring example of the compulsion of modern thinkers to face this monster. Freud was a great exception, and the success of his interpretation of the Oedipus myth has obscured the trend. Heidegger was the other great exception, though with far less influence on interpretation of the Oedipus myth.[56] Referring to a single text, Sophocles' *Oedipus the King*, and not to the motifs of the myth but to the plot of the tragedy, Heidegger took the blind Oedipus' emergence from the palace as exemplifying "the unity and conflict of being and appearance" in pre-Socratic metaphysics. "The way from the radiant beginning to the gruesome end is one struggle between appearance (concealment and distortion) and unconcealment (being)."[57] Elsewhere, Hegel's redirection of thought to the Sphinx episode continued to have repercussions in the twentieth century. Though Freud sidestepped the Sphinx, his early follower, Otto Rank, did not. In 1912, in a work of formidable learning on the incest theme in literature and myth, he described the Sphinx as a doubling of the mother, "intended to effect a splitting off of certain objectionable traits in the mother."[58] The modern iconographical tradition of the Sphinx which began with Ingres continued on past Max Ernst (cf. see pp. 102, 106). Amongst other works, one can name Giorgio de Chirico's painting *The Sphinx Questioning Oedipus* (1966), Pablo Picasso's drawing *Oedipus and the Sphinx* (1972), and Francis Bacon's painting *Oedipus and the Sphinx after Ingres* (1983).

The Sphinx looms large in the most important conceptual work on Oedipus of the second half of the twentieth century. In his "Dahlem Lectures" of 1972, "arbeiten mit ödipus" ("work with oedipus"), delivered at the Free University of Berlin, Klaus Heinrich's premise was that to work with Oedipus is to work with repression, which he regarded as the chief ill of contemporary society (his lectures often refer to the Berlin of his day), of the academic disciplines, and indeed of the history of Western philosophy. As a Marxist theologian, his goal was to reach behind the repressiveness of the Western philosophic tradition, which had begun, in Plato and Aristotle, with a denial of its mythical inheritance. He would reach back to non-repression through material offered by world religions, including, especially, ancient Greek myth. In his fifth lecture of 1972, he argues that Sophocles' tragedy in effect denies that Oedipus' answer, "man," has really solved the riddle and thus mocks the kind of definition of man which Sophocles sees emerging in contemporary philosophy. (Heinrich refers to Plato's later "two-footed featherless biped" and the cynic Diogenes' mockery thereof [Diogenes Laertius 6.40].) The tragedian "uses the riddle of the Sphinx . . . to criticize philosophy as a form of enlightenment which . . . represses the dimension which matters if one really . . . wants self-understanding."[59] For Heinrich, the Sphinx represents some ineluctable matriarchal power, though his larger concept of the unrepressed, the gravamen of his voluminous lectures, cannot be reduced to the Theban monster.

Two other thinkers, workers on the Oedipus myth, who likewise can be discussed only at a length far shorter than their thought deserves, are Jean-Joseph Goux and Giorgio Agamben. For both, Hegel is a conceptual point of departure; for both, Oedipus marks a turning point in human history, as in Hegel, but not in Hegel's sense. In the Italian philosopher, Hölderlin seems to rejoin Hegel in the notion that "the sin of Oedipus is not so much incest as it is hubris toward the power of the symbol in general [as represented in his solving the riddle of the Sphinx]."[60] Goux's title, *Oedipus, Philosopher*, epitomizes the Hegelian tradition, against which Heinrich was reacting. Goux discusses the Oedipus myth against the background of a precisely defined mono-myth of the Greek hero (represented by Jason, Bellerophon, and Perseus in particular), concentrating on the differences, especially clear in the Sphinx episode. Oedipus' monster-slaying, unlike that of the other heroes, is not imposed by a king; does not receive divine aid; and does not use force. To the Sphinx episode as a mythical anomaly, corresponds a ritual anomaly. The Sphinx ought to have been part of an initiation of the young hero, but the initiation fails, and indeed the Oedipus myth amounts to a tragedy of failed initiation. Oedipus lines up with Socrates, another anti-traditional autodidact, and takes the first step in the direction of Cartesian subjectivity. Now everyone has "to respond individually to the Sphinx through the insurrection of an autocentered 'I' that has suppressed her dangerous dimension."[61] One is inevitably reminded of Gide's Oedipus.

A common denominator of the Sphinx-interpretation of the three thinkers just considered is her matriarchal or primordial female nature (as in Propp, though his agenda was far different.) The resemblance of Friedrich Dürrenmatt's Sphinx to the one which has emerged in twentieth-century conceptual work on the Oedipus myth seems like a coincidence. Or is he deliberately turning this phase of work on the myth into a joke, as von Platen did with the Romantic Oedipus? In Dürrenmatt's radio-play *The Death of the Pythia*, Laius impregnated Hippodameia, the wife of Pelops (whose son Laius raped [cf. p. 16]). She gave birth to the Sphinx, who was raised by a priestess of Hermes. After the death of this priestess, the Sphinx withdrew to Mt. Cithaeron, where she raised lionesses, to protect herself from her father. Nevertheless, Laius entered her temple with his charioteer Polyphontes, who raped her. She gave birth to a son, also called Oedipus, at the same time Jocasta did. Laius gave orders that the

Sphinx's son should be exposed along with Jocasta's. A shepherd arrived at the Sphinx's temple with Jocasta's son, and, under the influence of drink, revealed that Jocasta had bribed him to hand her son over to a shepherd in the employ of the king of Corinth. While the shepherd was asleep, the Sphinx threw Jocasta's son to the lionesses, pierced the heels of her own son, and in the morning gave him to the shepherd. Oedipus grew up in Corinth knowing from the first that Polybus and Merope were his foster-parents. He went to Delphi to find out who his natural parents were and received the oracle, as in Sophocles. He assumed that any adult male he killed would be his father, and, when he killed Laius at the crossroads, he assumed that Laius was his father. He also killed Laius' charioteer Polyphontes, who was in fact his father. Next encountering the Sphinx, he solved her riddle and became her lover. Neither knew the identity of the other, but the growing restiveness of the lionesses showed that something was amiss. The Sphinx learned the truth from Delphi but was soon devoured by the lionesses. Oedipus continued to Thebes and married Jocasta, who he thought was his mother. He was glad to kill his father and marry his mother because he hated them both and wanted revenge.

OVERVIEW

With the Sphinx as the mother of Oedipus, one reaches a culmination of the modern tendency, beginning with Hegel and with Ingres, to make the Sphinx episode the central one in the Oedipus myth. This tendency appears most clearly in art but finds expression in all kinds of work on the myth, almost compulsively in Lévi-Strauss. The curious exception to this rule is Freud. No element in the Oedipus Complex corresponds to the hero's solving of the riddle. Freud's various references to the riddle itself are rather obscure, at least to present-day readers, and require research in order to be understood. Nevertheless, the success of the Oedipus Complex was an undoubted boost to the already strong forward movement of the myth, as the prestige of Aristotle was in the Renaissance.

CONCLUSIONS AND CONTINUATIONS

In ancient Greece, Oedipus is the accursed and polluted transgressor, whose curse passes on through the generations. At the same time, at least in Sophocles' *Oedipus at Colonus*, he is finally purified and is transfigured in death. In this tragedy, to quote more fully a passage of Hegel partly quoted earlier: "[A] god calls him . . .; his blind eyes are transfigured and clear; his bones become a salvation and safeguard of the state that received him as friend and guest. This transfiguration in death is for us, as for him, a visible reconciliation within his own self and personality."[1] It was the almost modern inwardness of this reconciliation – an inner peace – which struck Hegel, and, in the same breath with the words just quoted, he had to deny their obvious Christian implications. It was not a matter of the eternal bliss of Oedipus' soul. And yet, in the Middle Ages, implicitly in the "Planctus" and explicitly in Oedipus' avatars Gregory and Judas, it was the question of the efficacy of penance which the crimes of the Oedipal figure raised. Could any penance be sufficient? Could God forgive these enormities? The answer to these questions was yes, even if, as in the case of Andrew, the sinner also raped nuns and killed priests. Except for his despair, even Judas could have been redeemed. Such was the power of God's forgiveness. The "holy sinner" of the Middle Ages became the enlightened sinner of the eighteenth century, who saw his reason and virtue defeated by irrational forces but not annulled. The enlightened sinner became the transfigured sinner of the Romantic and modern periods, whose crimes amounted to a sacrifice necessary to some further stage of his own or, symbolically, of mankind's progress. In Nietzsche's words,

The noble man does not sin, the profound poet (Sophocles) wants to tell us: all law, all natural order, even the moral world may be destroyed by his actions, but precisely through these actions a higher enchanted circle of effects is drawn, which build a new world on the ruins of the old overturned one.[2]

CHARACTER OF OEDIPUS

Recapitulating the history of the Oedipus myth in these terms might make it seem that the myth is about the character of Oedipus, an exploration of his character. It is not. The myth or story is primary, and the character of Oedipus is an inference from the story, an inference obviously differing from time to time and from place to place. Only in the modern period does a certain reorientation begin, at least in conceptual work on the myth, and the events of the myth are construed in relation to the subjectivity of Oedipus, to his inner mental or emotional state. In the preceding chapter, Hegel's Oedipus was taken to mark the turning point, an Oedipus who stood for subjectivity in the sense of a newly won self-consciousness. Freud is the culmination of the modern tendency. The ultimate inwardness of the hero is that his deeds become only desires, and his desires are unconscious.

The tendency to locate the meaning of the myth in the subjectivity (to use the term now in a sense including a whole range of mental experience, from unconscious to intellectual) of Oedipus appears again and again in conceptual and scholarly work on the Oedipus myth, not only in psychoanalytic interpretation. In perhaps the most often cited article by a classical scholar on Sophocles' *Oedipus the King*, E.R. Dodds wrote: "To me personally Oedipus is a kind of symbol of the human intelligence which cannot rest until it has solved all the riddles. . . ."[3] It is quite possible to take the opposite view of Oedipus' intelligence while preserving the same orientation toward the subjectivity of the hero. Jonathan Lear writes:

Oedipus' fundamental mistake lies in his assumption that meaning is transparent to human reason. In horrified response to the Delphic oracle, Oedipus flees the people he (mistakenly) believes to be his parents. . . . [T]his scenario is possible only because Oedipus assumes he understands the situation, that the meaning

of the oracle is immediately available to his conscious understanding. . . . Oedipus'
mistake, in essence, is to ignore unconscious meaning.[4]

The two interpreters of Oedipus just quoted have something else in
common. Though both start from Sophocles' *Oedipus the King*, by the
time they reach their conclusions, they are talking about a hyposta-
tized Oedipus, that Oedipus referred to in the introduction to this
book who has come to have an existence apart from any of his instan-
tiations in any particular work on his myth. Gilles Deleuze and Felix
Guattari, the authors of *Anti-Oedipus: Capitalism and Schizophrenia*,
are another example of this tendency. They specifically oppose
Freud's claim to represent unconscious desire in terms of the Oedipus
Complex, but in their book, as their translators are obliged to explain,
". . . the term Oedipus has many widely varying connotations. . . .
It refers not only to the Greek myth of Oedipus and to the Oedipus
complex as defined by classical psychoanalysis, but also to Oedipal
mechanisms, processes, and structures."[5] In short, "Oedipus," even
when a particular thinker's Oedipus is in question, becomes a larger,
apparently autonomous figure.

The subjectivity of Oedipus is in fact a lacuna in the myth, one
which modern work on the myth attempts to fill. Benjamin, in his
review of André Gide's *Oedipus* (1932), saw the difference between the
ancient and the modern conceptions of Oedipus precisely in this
shift of emphasis from the outer to the inner man. He observed of
Gide's Oedipus that for the first time "*Oedipus has won speech.* The
Sophoclean Oedipus is in fact dumb, almost dumb." The very speech,
says Benjamin, in which Oedipus describes the consequences of his
incestuous marriage (1403–8), is precisely the one in which his inner
dimension ("*sein Inneres*") becomes dumb. Benjamin also quotes the
part of the same speech in which Oedipus says that, if he could shut
off his ears, as he has blinded himself, he would do so (1386–89).[6] He
would like to silence and still every inner reaction to his crimes. Gide,
then, to modernize the tragedy, has located and filled a lacuna of
silence.

VIRTUAL SPACES

One could say that Gide is only reusing a mechanism which creative work on the Oedipus myth has used ever since antiquity. Poets and others have again and again discerned virtual spaces in the myth and have moved to fill them. Sometimes it is simply a matter of reduplication. If the Sphinx posed a riddle, she could pose two or more riddles, as in Theodectes' *Oedipus* in the fourth century BC. If Teiresias was blind, he had to be led by someone, and that person could be his daughter. She had been known in archaic Theban epic. Seneca put her on stage in his *Oedipus* in the first century AD. The possibilities are much greater in a narrative form than in a tragedy, as the poet of the *Roman de Thèbes* demonstrated. Next to every female character, he could see a virtual space to be occupied by a lover. Genealogies are, of course, full of virtual spaces. Corneille can give Laius and Jocasta a daughter, Dirce, and, beside Dirce, yet another space opens up – for a lover, Theseus. The period between Oedipus' departure from Thebes and his arrival at Colonus is a large open space in the ancient myth. Cesare Pavese partly fills it with a dialogue between Oedipus and a beggar in "La Strada" (1947).[7] Henry Bauchau fills it with a novel, *Oedipus on the Road: A Novel* (1990). Oedipus' arrival at Colonus still leaves time for a long conversation with the Athenian king, Theseus, in André Gide's story "Theseus" (1946). Gide signals the lacuna in the story which he has found when he has Theseus say of himself and Oedipus: "*I am surprised that so little should have been said* about this meeting of our destinies at Colonus, this moment at the crossroads when our two careers confronted each other."[8] Likewise, Hélène Cixous, the feminist thinker, novelist, and playwright, in her libretto for the Oedipus opera by André Boucourechliev (1978), has Jocasta say: "There's a silence in my story. / Which I cannot forget any longer. That last silence of my father. / Night was falling. I was crossing the garden of childhood."[9] Cixous posits this silence, then replaces it with an account of the death of Jocasta's father.

Martha Graham's dance composition *Night Journey* originates in her perception of a virtual space in Sophocles' *Oedipus the King* (fig. 13). Toward the end of the tragedy, a messenger comes forth from the palace to report the suicide of Jocasta and the self-blinding

Figure 13 Martha Graham and Erick Hawkins in Martha Graham's *Night Journey*. Photo by Arnold Eagle. Photo by permission of his estate and by courtesy of Martha Graham Resources.

of Oedipus. He describes how Jocasta went to the bedroom, called upon Laius, bewailed the bed in which she had conceived children by her own son, and then he says, "of how she died thereafter I have no further knowledge, for with a shout Oedipus burst in and because of him it was impossible to see her misfortune . . ." (1244–54). The program notes for the first performance (1947, Cambridge, MA) quote these lines and thus indicate precisely where Graham intervened. It was in the lapse of time between Jocasta's expressions of grief and her suicide. Graham's dance shows Jocasta reliving, in this interval, her relationship with Oedipus. In the erotic pas de deux, she is the controlling figure, the seducer, and, in Graham's retelling of the myth, Oedipus' self-blinding takes place before Jocasta hangs herself. Her death will be the climax. The virtual space which Graham detected opens into the story of the relationship of mother and son as wife and husband. It is a story which Pier Paolo Pasolini was to treat even more graphically in the medium of film in his *Oedipus Rex* (1967). His meditation on the first sexual encounter of Oedipus and Jocasta can be found in his screenplay.[10] It is a story on which Jean Anouilh dwells in his *Oedipus or the Lame King after Sophocles* (written 1978).[11] In the opening dialogue, husband and wife reminisce about the ups and downs of their relationship. Jocasta had married Laius at the age of twelve, and, as the chorus will explain, he amused himself with her body for only a short time before returning to his concubines. She would have murdered him if brigands had not done it for her. "She only became a woman in the arms of Oedipus."

REDUCTION AND AMPLIFICATION

When one speaks of new creative work on Sophocles' *Oedipus the King,* as with Anouilh's or any of the dramas following Corneille's, the metaphor of space can sometimes be usefully replaced with the concept of reduction and/or amplification of the model.[12] One can, for example, redescribe the dynamics of reception in Corneille as a reduction of one important role, Creon's, to zero and an amplification of the family of Laius and Jocasta to include a daughter. Péladan's

Oedipus and the Sphinx drastically reduces the ancient model by omitting the discovery and self-blinding. The ultimate reduction of *Oedipus the King* is perhaps that of Daniel Nussbaum, a freelance writer in Los Angeles. He retold the tragedy in the medium of the personalized vehicle license plates called "vanity plates" in the United States (fig. 14) – a kind of pop-literature. He explains his impulse: "[O]ne day, in a state of light hypnosis brought on by hours of freeway driving, I had a vision. In my mind's eye, all the vanity plates in California lined up and made sense, re-telling the key works of our civilization."[13]

Amplification of some aspect of the model is to be seen in nearly every new Oedipus tragedy from the seventeenth century on. Cocteau amplifies the encounter with the Sphinx (all of Act 2). Pasolini amplifies the parricide. Sophocles' Oedipus says of Laius and his attendants, "I kill them all" (813), and, except for the one who escaped unbeknownst to Oedipus, the other members of Laius' retinue remained faceless and forgotten down to Pasolini's time. He shows in detail Oedipus' murder of each of Laius' four guards (and the furtive departure from the scene by the one who will ultimately incriminate Oedipus). In the film, the murder of Laius is thus the climax of a fully amplified episode.

Dryden and Voltaire criticize Corneille's subplot, but retain the amplified role which he gave to Jocasta. Corneille in fact initiates a refocalization of Sophocles' tragedy on the wife and mother of Oedipus. With Lauraguais' *Jocasta* (1781), the mother and wife of Oedipus receives equal billing. This new enlargement of the role of Jocasta within the Sophoclean model, distinct from the importance which she always had in the Thebaid tradition, persists through the nineteenth-century reorientation of reception and on to the present. The fanfare which accompanies the entrance of Jocasta in Igor Stravinsky's opera-oratorio loudly makes the point (1927). Both Act 1 and Act 3 ("The Wedding Night") of Jean Cocteau's *The Infernal Machine* (1934) are focused on Jocasta. Rabbe Enckell publishes his verse drama *Iokasta* in 1939. Martha Graham's modern dance composition *Night Journey*, discussed earlier, explores the amorous relationship of Oedipus and Jocasta, as does the opening dialogue of Oedipus and Jocasta in Anouilh's *Oedipus*. Charles Chaynes' opera *Jocasta* (1993) continues the trend.[14]

Oedipus the king (of the road)

ONCEPON ATIME LONG AGO IN THEBES IMKING. OEDIPUS DAKING. LVMYMRS. LVMYKIDS. THEBENS THINK OEDDY ISCOOL. NOPROBS.

OKAY MAYBE THEREZZ 1LITL1. MOTHER WHERERU? WHEREAT MYDAD? NOCALLZ NEVER. HAVENOT ACLUE. INMYMIND IWNDER WHOAMI? IMUST FINDEM.

JO MYWIFE GOES, "OED DONT USEE? WERHAPI NO LETITB." IGO "NOWAY. IAMBOSS. DONTU TELLME MYLIFE. INEED MYMOM. II WILLL FINDHER. FIND BOTHOF THEM."

SOI START SEEKING DATRUTH ABOUT WHO IAM. ITGOEZ ULTRAAA SLOWE. THE SPHYNXS RIDDLE WAS ACINCH BUT NOTTHIZ.

SUNLEE WEHEAR SHOCKING NEWS. WHEN IWASA TINY1 THISGRE8 4 SEER SED IWOOD OFF MY ROYAL OLDMAN THEN MARREE MYMAMA. SICKO RUBBISH, NESTPAS? WHOWHO COULDBE SOGONE? STILL MOMNDAD SENT MEEEEE AWAY. MEE ABABI AWAAAY.

NOWWWWW GETTHIZ. MANY MOONS GOBY. IMEET THISGUY ONATRIP. WEDOO RUMBLE. WHOKNEW? ILEFTMY POP ONE DEDMAN.

UGET DAFOTO. MAJR TSURIS. JOJO MYHONEE, MYSQEEZ, MYLAMBY, MIAMOR, MYCUTEE. JOJOY IZZ MYMOMY.

YEGODS WHYMEE? YMEYYME? LIFSUX. IAMBAD, IAMBADD, IMSOBAD. STOPNOW THIS HEDAKE. THIS FLESH DUZ STINK. ITZ 2MUCH PAYNE 4ONE2C. TAKEGOD MYEYES! AIEEEEE!

Figure 14 "Oedipus", pp. 24–6 from PL8SPK:CALIFORNIA VANITY PLATES RETELL THE CLASSICS by DANIEL NUSSBAUM. Copyright © 1994 by Daniel Nussbaum. Reprinted by permission of HarperCollins Publishers.

CONCEPTUAL WORK ON THE OEDIPUS MYTH

Conceptual work on the Oedipus myth in the modern period has been guided, in relation to the object which it intends to explain, by the same principle of more and less. Its object is not the same as that of creative work, however. Seeking a higher level of generality, conceptual work does not interpret any one instantiation of the myth, for example, Sophocles' *Oedipus the King*, but abstracts the story and isolates certain motifs. Though Hegel spoke eloquently of Oedipus' inner reconciliation in the second of Sophocles' Oedipus tragedies, it is fair to say that for him the riddle-solving epitomized the myth. Hegel's choice of this single motif as exemplifying the newly won consciousness of Oedipus founded a philosophical tradition of work on the Oedipus myth which has continued up to the present. It includes Nietzsche's "secret trinity of these fateful deeds [i.e., riddle-solving, parricide, incest]."[15] It continues with Heinrich, Goux, and Agamben.

Freud focuses on parricide and incest, ultimately, in *Totem and Taboo*, reducing the myth to the former of these two motifs. Lévi-Strauss, for whom no motif has any meaning in itself, vastly expands the dimensions of the myth to take in everything from Cadmus, the founder of Thebes, to the conflict between Oedipus' sons. Propp, like Freud and Lévi-Strauss, explains the myth in terms of its origin. Whereas for Freud it is incest dreams going back to the primal horde, and for Lévi-Strauss it is the overcoming of a cognitive dilemma, for Propp it is the vast historical change from one political order to another. Propp uses folklore comparatively to reach this conclusion, but he does not stop with a historical explanation. He shows that the possibility of recasting the myth as a tragedy depended entirely on the amplification of the motif of discovery or recognition, which comes easily, with no effort on the hero's part, in folklore (and in the version of the myth in Homer's *Odyssey*, where "straightway the gods made it known amongst men"). He shows the unity of the two parts of the myth represented by Sophocles' two Oedipus tragedies, which has been corroborated by scholarly work on this matter.[16]

Conceptual work on the Oedipus myth in the twentieth century has thus left three choices. In the one represented by the Hegelian tradition, the myth is about the subjectivity of Oedipus. Lévi-Strauss' interpretation cannot be accommodated to this tradition because Oedipus' riddle-solving counts for nothing in itself. The myth has to do with cognition but the cognition belongs to the society as a whole which tells the myth and for which the myth solves a problem. Lévi-Strauss thus also historicizes the myth. The problem it once solved no longer exists, and the myth no longer has its historical function. In Propp's interpretation, the Oedipus myth is also historicized, its origin removed to a very remote period in human history in which one political order replaced another. The vast, lasting change had to do with the transmission of political power from one generation to the next. The myth originated in and is still about power relations.

Freud at first seems quite remote from such a view. His discovery of childhood sexuality made possible a reconception of the crimes of Oedipus as childhood desires. Desire, desire for the mother, seems to be the cornerstone of the Oedipus Complex. It is not so simple. Freud never really says which, the sexual impulse directed toward the mother or the murderous wish against the father, comes first and, one assumes, provokes the other. In *Totem and Taboo* (1913) he speaks of the "father-complex," later correcting this phrase to "parental complex."[17] In the introduction to the second edition of *The Interpretation of Dreams*, he speaks of this book as "a portion of my own self-analysis, my reaction to my father's death – that is to say, to the most important event, the most poignant loss, of a man's life."[18] It is difficult not to link this statement to the death of the father in Freud's legend of the primal horde. Of that legend, again, one asks which is primary – the young males' aggression against the chief or their desire for the women whom he has in his control? Freud leaves open a political interpretation of the myth which can be assimilated to that of Propp, who saw, at its center, the acquisition of power or the succession to power. On the other hand, a statement like the one in *Introductory Lectures on Psychoanalysis* (1916–17) might make one think that desire for the mother is indeed primary,[19] and this understanding of the Oedipus Complex is certainly the prevailing one, as its expression in humor shows – Tom Lehrer's song "Oedipus Rex" (1950s) or Woody Allen's film "Oedipus Wrecks," a segment of *New York Stories* (1989), or Ted Hughes' poem about Oedipus, "Song for a Phallus," each stanza of which ends with the refrain "Mamma Mamma."[20]

INCOHERENCE

Within conceptual work on the Oedipus myth in the twentieth century, a certain incoherence sets in. While everyone who comes after him is obliged to face Freud, Lévi-Strauss does not know Propp's study of the Oedipus myth, nor does Goux, despite the fact that, in constructing a typology of a certain hero myth, Goux necessarily analyzes the motifs which Propp had analyzed.[21] Incoherence results not only from ignorance. It can be willful. Carl Robert, whose two-volume study of the Oedipus myth is considered the greatest work of classical scholarship on this subject, expresses only passing contempt for Hofmannsthal.[22] The classicist typically asks: what did the Oedipus myth mean in its own time? This question in and of itself rules out concern with its reception in later ages. Jean Bollack, for example, in his massive four-volume commentary on Sophocles' *Oedipus the King* (1990), makes it his goal to peel away the layers of distortion which this tragedy has acquired in the long history of its reception and to return to its original meaning.

Incoherence is necessarily even broader and deeper in creative work on the Oedipus myth. An artist works within the tradition of his or her medium. No one would ask, and it would be inappropriate to ask, if Francis Bacon (cf. p. 126) knew William Butler Yeats' translation of Sophocles' *Oedipus the King* (1928). Qu Xiasong, whose opera *Oedipus* premiered in 1993 in Stockholm, knew Stravinsky's *Oedipus Rex*,[23] but did he know Max Ernst's surrealist painting *Oedipus Rex*? Again, the question seems inappropriate. Qu's one-act chamber opera *The Death of Oedipus*, based on the second of Sophocles' Oedipus tragedies, which premiered in Amsterdam in 1994, is a Buddhist interpretation of the hero's death. Was Qu aware of Lee Breuer and Bob Telson's Christian version of the same tragedy, *The Gospel at Colonus* (premiere 1983), an oratorio set in a black Pentecostal service?[24] An incoherence begins to emerge even within a single artistic tradition. It may sometimes be ineluctable. Are the scores of the eighteenth- and early nineteenth-century operas on the subject of Oedipus at Colonus extant? If so, are they accessible to anyone but a resolute, well-funded researcher?

Ola Rotimi's *The Gods Are Not to Blame* (1971) is perhaps an extreme case of incoherence. Though Rotimi was a student of Western drama even before his time at Yale University in the 1960s, his rewriting of Sophocles' *Oedipus the King* seems oblivious of the rich history of the reception of this tragedy. He was guided by the exigencies of transposing the Sophoclean material into the conditions of the Yoruba tribe in pre-colonial Nigeria. Tribal customs and politics provided the new vocabulary of the myth, and Rotimi once said that the main purpose of this play was to warn against tribalism.[25] In a striking display of the irrelevance of authorial intention to reception, Rotimi's play went on to innumerable performances in times and venues in which the message concerning tribalism was inconspicuous at best.

INDIVIDUAL PERSPECTIVES ON THE TRADITION

Beyond the coherence of determinate literary histories, like those of Italian and French Oedipus drama, such coherence as Oedipus reception possesses lies in the particular perspective which the individual beholder happens to bring with him or her to any new work on the myth. In my perspective on Rotimi, the phenomenon of differently motivated parallels to other rewritings is striking. Like Corneille, but for completely different reasons, Rotimi deletes the role of Creon. Like Pasolini, again for completely different reasons, he dramatizes the parricide. Rotimi's amplification of the role of the Corinthian messenger (here Alaka) reminds of, but far surpasses, other dramatists' treatment of this character. Rotimi's deletion of the Sphinx, which lacked a Yoruba correlative, reminds yet again of the volatility of this troublesome creature. Such comparisons are, again, outside Rotimi's intention and perhaps outside his ken. But they belong to the beholder's experience, and this experience is the form which the tradition ultimately takes. But the history of reception is too long and too multifarious for anyone to grasp as a whole, and known unknowns qualify one's perceptions, for example, in my case, the Oedipus play, *No hay resistencia a los hados* ("You cannot resist the fates") by Alejandro Arboreda (1650–98). Equally abundant, no doubt, are the unknown unknowns, and, in these areas, critics of this book will wade in.

A historian of art or of music, a psychologist or an anthropologist would bring another perspective to Rotimi's play and would see things which I missed. Likewise, if any of these persons had written this book, it would give a far different picture of the history of the Oedipus reception. All books which make the desperate attempt to write the whole history will have only one thing in common. They will not find any conclusion in the material with which they have to deal. They will only find continuations. Somewhere, as I write, a philosopher or anthropologist or a thinker in some other field is seeking the meaning in the Oedipus myth which had escaped Freud and the others. Somewhere a painter or sculptor or composer is contemplating a revolutionary work. What should be the subject? Oedipus! A dramatist is putting pen to paper: the times demand a new rewriting of Sophocles' *Oedipus the King*. A new Sphinx is slouching or flying toward Thebes to be born. A new Oedipus is starting down the road on which he will meet her.

NOTES

INTRODUCING OEDIPUS

1 For the five figures see Holthusen 1960; for "work on myth," Blumenberg 1985.
2 Aarne and Thompson 1981.
3 See the introduction to Edmunds 1985 for a detailed comparative study of the motifs of folktale and ancient myth.
4 SE 4: 261–62.

1 OEDIPUS BEFORE TRAGEDY

1 And belongs to the same thematic complex as *algea*: Nagy [1979]1999: 74–75, 79–81.
2 Stesichorus fr. 222b.201, 215 Davies; Ibycus fr. S222 Davies. In a fragment of Hesiod's *Catalogue of Women*, Oedipus has the epithet *polykēdēs*. The noun from which this word comes, *kēdos*, usually occurs in the plural and means generally "troubles" or, more often, "funeral rites" or "mourning." So the epithet can be translated "of many troubles," with the connotation of sorrow for the deaths he has caused, his father's and his mother's (Hesiod fr. 193.4 M-W).
3 Perhaps attested already in the second millennium in a tablet from Knossos: Ventris and Chadwick 1956: 127, 306–7.
4 *FGrH* 16 F 10. Cf. de Kock 1961; de Kock 1962; Lloyd-Jones 2002.
5 Moret 1984.1: 64–65; Krauskopf 1994: 5 (item 40).
6 Moret 1984.1: 83–84; Krauskopf 1994: 8–9 (items 73–77).
7 Moret 1984.1: 90.

8 Moret 1984.1: 41 (item 36), 55–56, 175 (item 87); 1984.2: plates 23; 50–51.1; Krauskopf 1994: 4 (item 19); 6 (item 48). First publication of the earlier vase: Kreuzer 1992: 86–88 (item 91); she does not, however, print the inscriptions on the vase, and the riddle remains obscure. Thus my "perhaps." Time will tell.

9 Athenaeus 10.83; also *Anth. Pal.* 14.64.

10 The argument of Porzig 1953 for a forerunner of the riddle in Indo-European, the parent language of ancient Greek, is implausible. Cf. Katz forthcoming.

11 Sumatra: Damsté 1917: 231–32. Philippine Islands: Hart 1964: 233 (878). Sub-Saharan Africa: Fraser 1914: 171.

12 Schultz 1914: cols. 69–70; Hain 1966: 36–42; AT851A.

13 "Creon gives Oedipus the kingship and the wife of Laius, Oedipus' mother, Jocasta, from whom are born to him Phrastor and Laonytus, who die at the hands of Minyans and Erginus. [At this point there is apparently a lacuna in the narrative.] After a year came around, Oedipus marries Euryganeia, the daughter of Periphas, from whom are born to him Antigone and Ismene, whom Tydeus kills at a spring, and the spring is called Ismene after her. Sons are born to him from her [Euryganeia], Eteocles and Polynices. After Euryganeia died, Oedipus marries Astymedousa, the daughter of Sthenelus" (*FGrH* 3 F 95). On this version, unique in several ways, see Cingano 1992: 3–4, 9–10. The murder of Ismene by Tydeus is attested in the seventh-century poet Mimnermus (fr. 21 W²); cf. on Sophocles' *Antigone* in the following chapter.

14 The word for "died" might mean "died in battle," in which case Oedipus was certainly not blind and he would have been carrying on in heroic fashion. The word might, however, mean simply "died."

15 fr. 3 Bernabé = fr. 3 Davies = fr. 3 Loeb.

16 See Cingano 2003b on the significance of the distribution of the parts of the sacrificial victim.

17 fr. 2 Bernabé = fr. 2 Davies = fr. 2 Loeb.

18 An anonymous fragment of a tragedy or a comedy imitates or parodies the curse on the sons. In this fragment, Oedipus is explicitly blind (adesp. F 458 Snell-Kannicht).

19 Lévi-Strauss [1973]1976: ch. xiii.

20 From Lysimachus 382 *FGrH* F 2. Lysimachus was an Alexandrian historian (third–second c. BC).

21 324 *FGrH* F 62. The presence of Poliouchos Athena is not attested in Sophocles' Oedipus the King, but this inconsistency does not weaken the evidence for present purposes.

2 OEDIPUS ON STAGE

1 Achaeus; Philocles; Xenocles; Nicomachus. See Snell 1971 for testimonia, titles, and fragments, if any.

2 On ancient Greek pederasty see Halperin 1990, 1996.

3 This fr. is not included in Smyth 1963.

4 772–84. I have followed the text and the notes of Hutchinson 1985.

5 For an overview of Labdacid myth in Euripides see Aélion 1986: 29–92.

6 Cingano 2003a: 72 n. 15; Griffith 1999: 350–51 (on 1302–3).

7 The difference between Euripides (chariot) and Antimachus (horses) suggests that neither is borrowing from the other and that both are following the same tradition. It is of great interest that this same version of the parricide appears in Peisander (cf. Ch. 1) and also in the *Histories* of Nicolaus of Damascus (first c. BC), *FGrH* 90 F 8.

8 Robert 1915.1: 307; Krauskopf 1974: 97; Krauskopf 1994: 9 (item 85).

9 For a list of examples of blinding as punishment for sexual transgression see Devereux 1973; cf. Buxton 1980.

10 Bettini and Guidorizzi 2004: 104.

11 fr. *545a Kannicht. Trans. by Collard *et al.* 1995–2004.2: 119; cf. Collard 2005: 61–62.

12 frs. **185–90 Radt; translation in Lloyd-Jones 1996: 72–77.

13 Segal 2001.

14 Edmunds 1981b.

15 Burkert 1985: 111–14.

16 Aesch. *Sept.* 24–27; Soph. *Ant.* 988–1090; Eur. *Phoen.* 834–960, 1589–91; *Bacch.* 347 etc.

17 Oedipus comes into Cicero's *De Fato/On Fate* (44 BC) as one of the examples of fate used by the Stoic philosopher Chrysippus (ca. 280–207 BC) (30, 33; same name as that of the boy raped by Laius [cf. p. 16].

18 Aarne and Thompson 1981: 325.

19 *The Interpretation of Dreams* (1900) = SE 4: 262. Cf. *Introductory Lectures on Psychoanalysis* (1915–16) = SE 15: 208.

20 Edmunds 2002.

21 Propp [1944]1983: 83.

22 Edmunds 1996: 138–42. Some parts of the present discussion are adapted from these pages.

23 *FGrH* 324F62.

24 See Edmunds 1981b: 224 n. 12.

25 See Daly 1990: 138 and n. 43 on the verb *mēniō*.

26 This paragraph up to this point and the preceding paragraph are adapted from Edmunds 1996: 128–30.
27 Propp [1944]1983: 118. Cf. Edmunds 1985: 38–40.
28 On this, "one of the more baffling situations in Greek myth," see Gantz 1993: 512–14.
29 Parsons 1999; Katz forthcoming.

3 LATIN OEDIPUS

1 *De Finibus/On Moral Ends* (45 BC) 5.3. The work was composed in 45 BC; the dialogue is set in Athens in 79 BC.
2 Fr. 347, on which see Cèbe 1990.
3 For a systematic comparison of Seneca's tragedy with Sophocles' *Oedipus the King* see Miller 1917: 564–69.
4 On Argos, Thebes, and Athens as archetypes in the *Thebaid*, see Vessey 1982: 576–77.
5 For the liturgy: Palmer 1989: 58; for Augustine: Brown 1967: 38, 271–73, 412.
6 Reynolds 1983: 378–81, 394–96.
7 Schmidt 1978: 66 and Tschiedel 1978: 78 for the Christian Seneca. In this paragraph, I have relied on the chapters of Schmidt and Tschiedel just cited and on Blüher 1978: 138–39 and Wanke 1978: 174 for information on Antoni de Vilaragut.
8 Seneca's tragedies were not translated into a modern language – it was Catalan – until 1388. The translator was Antoni de Vilaragut.
9 Constans 1890. His version is 10,230 lines long. In the following, I cite the translation of Coley 1986. He translated the Constans edition.
10 The name Lactantius Placidus should probably be put in quotation marks: see Cameron 2004: 313–16.
11 As argued in Edmunds 1982, which has been substantiated by Punzi 1995: 175–230. As she points out (ibid.: 218), I should have included the Old Irish *Togail Tebe*. She discusses the two possible attestations of the preface, long considered lost, as in my article, at pp. 218–25.
12 Messerli 2002: 131 points out a couple of instances of accurate knowledge of the Sphinx.
13 On religion in the poem see Grout 1977. For an excellent short essay on the poem as a whole see Blumenfeld-Kosinski 1997: 19–30.
14 On the episode of Darius the Red see Baswell 2000: 36–39.
15 Auerbach [1946]1953: 131.

16 Erdmann and Ekwall 1930: 12–14.
17 See Messerli 2002: 57–68, 306–09.
18 Vitz and Gartner 1984.
19 Edmunds 1985: 61–62.
20 Edmunds 1985: 18–19, 36.
21 UK1, UK2, OR1, RS1, RS2 in Edmunds 1985.
22 Edmunds 1985: 188–92 (OR1).
23 Edmunds 1985: 79–88 (LT1).
24 Edmunds 1985: 61–65 (LT1, LT2).
25 Ohly [1976]1992: 29.
26 Again, I cite myself: Edmunds 1985.

4 REDISCOVERY OF SOPHOCLES

1 Mann 1996: 16 gives 1392 and speaks of it as a "key date."
2 Sandys 1906–8.2: 36; Reynolds and Wilson 1991: 147–48.
3 The numbers for Sophocles come from Borza 2003; for tragedies from Mastrocola 1996: 9–10. The generalization about the sixteenth century is based on Mastrocola 1996: 9–25, whose critical reflection (ibid.: 20–21) on Steiner 1986 is valuable.
4 Weinberg 1961.2: 953. Surveys of the history of the *Poetics* in the Renaissance: Sandys 1906–8.2: 133–35; Tigerstedt 1968 (fullest); Garin 1973 (reflections on Tigerstedt); Hutton 1982: 27–30; bibliography in Mastrocola 1996: 24 n. 18.
5 For Cinzio: Weinberg 1961.2: 913; for Cavalcanti: ibid.: 919; for Dolfini: ibid.: 943.
6 For humanist editions and university lectures see Borza 2003: 53–54 with his references.
7 Sandys 1906–8.2: 216–17. For a short history of the editions of Sophocles see Lloyd-Jones and Wilson 1990: 1–6.
8 Text of Anguillara's play, called simply *Edippo*, in Anguillara 1809. One of the dates I have seen for the performance is 1560. The publication was in 1565. Paduano 1994: 266–70; Mastrocola 1996: 99–112.
9 Cunliffe 1906: xxix.
10 Riccoboni 1996: 1–12; Schrade 1960 (includes Gabrieli's score); Weinberg 1961.2: 942–45; Gallo 1973; Gordon 1975; Vidal-Naquet 1981: 6–13 = Vidal-Naquet 1996: 13–31; Flashar 1991: 27–34. For further indications, see Flashar 1991: 319 n. 1. For a bibliography on Palladio and the theater at Vicenza, see Vidal-Naquet 1981: 23 n. 20 = Vidal-Naquet 1996: 19 n. 20.

11 Melanchthon 1834–60.3: 374 (no. 1579).

12 The song: Sachs 1884: 64–66; the play: Keller 1874: 29–53; the aphoristic poem (Spruchgedicht): Keller and Goetze 1892: 478–82. A complete investigation of Sachs' sources for this myth is still lacking. Abele 1899: 95–96 is the starting point.

13 For this devil literature see Osborn 1893.

14 1984: 280–81. See p. 153 for comments on Racine's *La Thébaïde*.

15 For Tesauro, see Paduano 1994: 285–88. In this paragraph I have relied on Biet 1994a and Biet 1999. For Rotrou, see Biet 1994b: 177–99. The first two acts cover the ancient *Thebaid*, the next three the ancient *Antigone*. I believe that the references of Steiner 1984 to a *Thébaïde* by Rotrou are to his *Antigone*.

16 Theile 1975: 39.

17 "Au Lecteur"/"To the Reader" and "Examen"/"Examination" in Corneille 1987: 17–21. Text of tragedy: ibid.: 22–93; discussion and notes: ibid.: 1366–81.

18 See Biet 1994b: 204–12.

19 Corneille 1987: 1370.

20 Guffey and Roper 1984: 113–215 (text), 441–96 (valuable discussion and notes); Biet 1994b: 223–35.

21 Guffey and Roper 1984: 116.

22 Cf. Biet 1994b: 233–35.

23 Smollett 1901.16: 148–209; repr. in Sanderson and Zimmerman, ed. 1968: 105–43.

24 For the periodization, I have followed Vidal-Naquet 1981: 3; Biet 1999. For a list of works see the "corpus" in Biet 1994b: 17–18. I do not mean to imply that no Oedipus tragedies were written outside of France. See Paduano 1994: V–VI for an international list. The preponderance, however, is French. For the Count of Lauraguais, see Vidal-Naquet 1981: 16; Biet 1994b: 299–300. Text of Voltaire's play: 1820.

25 Biet 1994b: 268–72.

26 Biet 1994b: 131–37 for Gaillard; ibid.: 467 for bibliographical information on the essay.

5 THE INWARD TURN

1 For a useful survey see Kocziszky 1995. In my discussion of Hegel, I have relied on Flashar 1996.

2 "In Lovely Blueness . . ." is a prose-poem taken from the novel *Phaethon* (1823) by Wilhelm Waiblinger, who used his friend Hölderlin as a model

for the character Phaethon. It is uncertain whether the prose-poem is completely Waiblinger's or based on notes of Hölderlin in Waiblinger's possession. (The oft-quoted sentence, "Oedipus has perhaps an eye too many," is from this prose-poem.) The discussion of "In Lovely Blueness . . ." by Rudnytsky 1987: 129–30 is necessarily qualified by these bibliographic considerations.

3 Text of Hölderlin's translation: Hölderlin 1994: 787–848. The notes: Hölderlin 1994: 849–57. My quotations from the notes: ibid.: 851–52. Also, ibid., "God is nothing but time." The explication of these notes by Steiner 1986: 77–80 is valuable. English translation of Hölderlin's translation, including the notes: Hölderlin 2001.

4 Nietzsche [1872]2000: 32 (section 4). Cf. Rudnytsky 1987: 121–30. Caution is necessary concerning Rudnytsky's estimate of Hölderlin's knowledge of Greek (ibid.: 128): cf. Schadewalt 1996.

5 Hegel 1987: 746–47, 639.

6 Hegel 1975: 360–61.

7 Schlegel [1846]1996: 163 = Schlegel 1846: 101.

8 von Platen 1895. For a summary of the play: Paduano 1994: 348–49.

9 Hegel 1975: 1219.

10 Hegel 1975: 1213–14; cf. 213–14.

11 Flashar 2001 is a remarkable study of the cultural background, the composition, the performance, and the later reception of the music.

12 Rubin 1973.

13 Hegel 1975: 1219 (my emphasis).

14 Hegel 1975: 1219.

15 Nietzsche [1872]2000: 54–55 (section 9).

16 References to *The Birth of Tragedy* are to §22 of the work itself and to §6 of the preface to the second edition.

17 Wagner [1868]1913.

18 Wagner [1868]1913.1: 317–41. Citations of this chapter are by the numbered sections.

19 See the magisterial study of the Sphinx in Greek art by Moret 1984; Krauskopf 1974; Krauskopf 1994.

20 For Ingres: Rubin 1979; Cherqui 1989; Posèq 2001. For Ernst: Chadwick 1975. For a speculative essay on Oedipus in nineteenth-century art, Wat and Absalon 1999.

21 Cavafy 1976: 196.

22 On Moreau: Praz 1967: 295–96. It is possible, as Halm-Tisserant 1981 argues, that Moreau's amorous Sphinx was inspired by ancient iconography, i.e., by his perception of such a Sphinx in that iconography. Moret 1984: 11

shows that, for the ancients, there was no amorous Sphinx. On the Oedipus figure in Moreau as an allusion to Christ's deposition from the cross see Uerscheln 1993: 34.

23 Text of the play: Péladan 1903. Discussion: Paduano 1994: 356–61.

24 The translation, like the translated passages of Hofmannsthal's play are those of Gertrude Schoenbohm in Kallich, MacLeish, and Schoenbohm, eds 1968. The German text of the play can be found in the massive variorum edition: Hofmannsthal 1983.

25 The notes are discussed by Hederer 1960: 141–60.

26 The quotations in this paragraph are from Schoenbohm (cf. n. 24 above) in Kallich *et al.* 1968: 157 and 163.

27 SE 1: 265–66.

28 SE 4: 261–63.

29 Influences in Freud's life: Rudnytsky 1987: 3–89. History of the psycho-analytic movement: Ellenberger 1970. Feminist critique of Freud: Kurzweil 1995. Controversy in the 1980s: Malcolm 1984; Masson 1985. Anti-Oedipus: Deleuze and Guattari 1983; Holland 1999. It should be noted that the most famous psychoanalyst and theoretician of psychoanalysis after Freud, Jacques Lacan (1901–81), belongs to the history of the psychoanalytic movement, not to the history of the reception of the Oedipus myth.

30 SE 20: 37.

31 SE 4: 263.

32 In a footnote to *Totem and Taboo* (1913) he would comment on blinding as "a substitution [for castration] that occurs, too, in the myth of Oedipus" (SE 13: 130 n. 1).

33 SE 4: 261.

34 SE 7.194–95; cf. 9.135, 10.133, 16.318, 20. 37.

35 Probably it is the riddle found in Aarne 1918–20: nos. 66, 173, 179, 212, which Róheim 1934: 21 summarizes as follows: "Two people lie in one bed. The observer first sees four legs (i.e., the father on all fours), then the two outstretched legs of the mother, and finally one leg which . . . mysteriously disappears." Cf. Rokem 1996.

36 SE 4: 262; cf. SE 15: 208.

37 SE 20: 214, my emphasis.

38 SE 10: 41–43.

39 For the story of Enescu's *Oedipe*, see Malcolm 1990: 139–59.

40 Lists can be found in Astier 1974: 235–38; Edmunds 1991 (highly selective but includes items not in the other lists); Reid 1993; Rösch-von der Heyde 1999; Odagiri 2001: 255–57. For Oedipus and the Sphinx, see the database on Sara Harrington's webpage (see Further Reading).

41 Nice 1991: 9; Walsh 1993: 93–95.

42 Stravinsky on his choice of Latin: Stravinsky 1936: 196, 201–2, 206. Stravinsky in his old age: Stravinsky and Craft 1963: 14–15 (with comment also on free accentuation of words). On Daniélou's Latinity: Farrell 2001: 117–23. For a detailed history of the composition of *Oedipus Rex*: Walsh 1993: 1–10.

43 Cocteau 1959.1: 211: ". . . ne sachant comment m'apprendre qu'il écrivait un *Oedipe* après les miens, il me dit en détachant les syllables: Il y a une véritable Oedipémie." Odagiri 2001: 182 quotes another form of the remark, from Campagne 1989: 59. I have not seen Campagne.

44 Odagiri 2001: 219–30; Paduano 1994: 177–83.

45 Cocteau 1991: 21–27 (with photographs)= Cocteau 1956: 180–84.

46 Cf. Weir 1991: 20.

47 Cocteau 1952: 52.

48 Nightmare: 1952: 192. Union of mother and son: ibid.: 198.

49 Cocteau 1971: vii.

50 Gide 1948.2: 298 (Feb. 4, 1922), 347 (Jan. 7, 1924), 351 (June 19, 1924).

51 Propp [1944]1983.

52 On Propp in this period in the Soviet Union, see Liberman's introduction to Propp 1984: ix–xv. Propp's historical interpretation of the folktale assumed much larger proportions in Propp [1946]1983. References to the works of Marx and Engels in the first chapter make clear Propp's ideological affiliations.

53 Lévi-Strauss [1985]1988: 186.

54 Quotations in this and the preceding paragraph from Lévi-Strauss [1955]1967: 212.

55 Quotations in this paragraph are in order from Lévi-Strauss [1973]1976: 25, 22. (The chapter here cited goes back to a lecture delivered in 1960.)

56 Heidegger [1953]1961: 90–92.

57 Heidegger [1953]1961: 90.

58 [1912]1992: 216, 220. A modern Greek folktale in which a queen who sits on a cliff near Thebes is the riddler figures in his argument. Translation and discussion in Edmunds 1981a: 6–11.

59 Heinrich 1993: 135.

60 Agamben 1993: 135–40, 144–45. The quotation is from p. 138.

61 Goux 1992: 54, 201.

CONCLUSIONS AND CONTINUATIONS

1 Hegel 1975: 1219.
2 Nietzsche [1872]2000: 54 (section 9).
3 Dodds 1966: 48.
4 Lear 1998: 29.
5 Deleuze and Guattari 1983: n. 3.
6 Benjamin [1931–32]1966, his emphasis.
7 Translation in Pavese 1965.
8 Gide 1950: 105. My emphasis.
9 Cixous 1978: 17.
10 Pasolini 1971: 61.
11 Anouilh 1986.
12 Frick 1998: 336 (general statement), ibid.: 345–57 (on Gide), ibid.: 358–63 (Corneille and Voltaire); ibid.: 366–70 (Cocteau).
13 Nussbaum 1994: preface (unpaginated).
14 This paragraph started from Odagiri 2001: 127–38.
15 Nietzsche [1872]2000: 54–55 (section 9).
16 Seidensticker 1972.
17 SE 13: 157.
18 SE 4.
19 SE 16: 329.
20 Hughes 2003: 248.
21 Lévi-Strauss knew Propp's *Morphology of the Folktale* (Propp [1928]1968) and discussed it in "Structure and Form: Reflections on a Work by Vladimir Propp," an article published in 1960: Lévi-Strauss [1973]1976: 115–45. Goux cites Propp three times but never the work on Oedipus and folklore: 1993: 212 n. 1 (Propp [1928]1968: 213), ch. 3 n. 2 (Propp [1946]1983: 315), 214 n. 3 (Propp [1946]1983: 319).
22 Robert 1915.1: 494.
23 So I infer from a general reference which Qu makes in an interview with Glen Saunders in Saunders 1996: 56.
24 Breuer and Telson 1989. A CD of the music was available at the time of the writing of this book; a PBS video recording of a performance was out of print.
25 Conradie 1994: 34–35.

FURTHER READING

Complete bibliographical information for these suggestions appears in Works Cited (pp. 157–68). For more detail on any ancient author or topic, *The Oxford Classical Dictionary*, 3rd ed., is the first place to look (hereafter *OCD*). The online database "Perseus" (http://www. perseus.tufts.edu) contains an enormous amount of information on ancient Greece and Rome.

I OEDIPUS BEFORE TRAGEDY

For an excellent narrative summary of all of Theban myth, unencumbered by references and notes, see Richard Martin's *Myths of the Ancient Greeks*. At the other extreme, a motif-by-motif survey of the ancient evidence for the Oedipus myth can be found in my *Oedipus: The Ancient Legend and its Later Analogues* (pp. 7–17). Translation of most of the fragmentary material from which the pre-tragic myth has to be reconstructed can be found in West's Loeb (see "Loeb" in Abbreviations, p. 170). For hero cult in general, see Emily Kearns' article in *OCD* and for the cult of Oedipus at Colonus in particular her *The Heroes of Attica*. For the Sphinx, Albert Schachter's article in *OCD*. In addition to the maps in this book, for a map of ancient central Greece with links from the place names to information about the places, go to http://www.plato-dialogues.org/tools/gr_south.htm (accessed 1/06).

2 OEDIPUS ON STAGE: FIFTH-CENTURY TRAGEDY

Numerous translations of the Theban tragedies are available. For studying the myth, one wants something rather faithful to the original. For Aeschylus' *Seven*, there is Gregory Nagy's revision of E.D.A. Morshead's translation at http://www.courses.dce.harvard.edu/~ clase116/txt_sevenagainst.html (accessed 1/06). The most recent offering from a major publisher is by Anthony Hecht and Helen Bacon, in Oxford University Press' ongoing series,"Greek Tragedy in New Translations," which pairs a distinguished classicist and a distinguished poet. For the fragments of Aeschylus' Theban trilogy, a translation is available in Smyth's Loeb, volume 2. The meager fragments of his *Oedipus*, with cross-references to fragments which other editors have assigned to this play, are at pp. 437–39.

For Sophocles' Theban plays, Ruby Blundell's *Sophocles: The Theban Plays: Antigone, King Oidipous, Oidipous at Colonus* meets the criterion of fidelity, and also has a helpful introduction. In the Oxford series, one has an *Oedipus the King* by Stephen Berg and Diskin Clay, an *Oedipus at Colonus* by Eamon Grennan and Rachel Kitzinger, and an *Antigone* by the unpaired Richard Emil Braun.

For leads to interpretation of *Oedipus the King*, Charles Segal's *Oedipus Tyrannus: Tragic Heroism and the Limits of Knowledge* is a good place to start. His "Selected Bibliography" (pp. 167–74) includes an indication of the contents of each of the works he cites. A particular problem for modern readers is the oracles in this play, which, in effect, begins with the oracle concerning the plague which Creon brings from Delphi. To learn more about the Delphic oracle, see Joseph Fontenrose's *The Delphic Oracle*. The oracle at the beginning of the play leads to the summoning of Teiresias and a long angry scene, for which I recommend my own article "The Teiresias Scene in Sophocles' *Oedipus Tyrannus*."

For Euripides, the only complete tragedy which is relevant is *Phoenician Women*. The translation in volume 5 of the Loeb Euripides by David Kovacs is the one which best meets the criterion of fidelity which I am applying. There is also a translation by Peter Burian and Brian Swann in the Oxford series mentioned above. Fragments of the lost Theban plays of Euripides can be found in a recent translation by Christopher Collard.

A theme which I have emphasized, the curse on the Labdacids, is discussed by Hugh Lloyd-Jones in *The Justice of Zeus*, pp. 113–24.

3 LATIN OEDIPUS: ROME AND THE MIDDLE AGES

For both Seneca and Statius excellent new Loeb translations are available. For the former, that of John G. Fitch, *Seneca*, vols. 8–9, with excellent introductions to the individual plays (2002–4). In Chapter Three, I cited the older Loeb Seneca of Frank J. Miller, for the reason given in the relevant endnote. Seneca is currently experiencing an upsurge, which will perhaps come to be reflected in Oedipus reception. For Statius, one has the new translation by D.R. Shackleton Bailey. The first of the two volumes has an important essay by Kathleen M. Coleman on recent scholarship on the epic. The most recent translation of the *Roman de Thèbes* is that of Coley. Baswell, in *The Cambridge Companion to Medieval Romance*, provides a helpful introduction. The best book on the literary tradition of Oedipus in the Middle Ages is in Italian, Punzi's. For the popular tradition, there are the texts in my collection, *Oedipus: The Ancient Legend and its Later Analogues*.

4 REDISCOVERY OF SOPHOCLES: FROM THE RENAISSANCE TO THE EIGHTEENTH CENTURY

Nicholas Mann's essay, "The Origins of Humanism," in *The Cambridge Companion to Renaissance Humanism*, provides a good general introduction to the period in which Sophocles arrives in Italy. Robert Garland's chapter, "Refugees and Publishers," in *Surviving Greek Tragedy*, tells the story in more detail. The only book dedicated entirely to the sixteenth-century Oedipus is in Italian (Mastrocola). My account plays down Seneca. For a corrective, see Charlton, *The Senecan Tradition in Renaissance Tragedy*. The major works on Oedipus in France in the seventeenth and eighteenth centuries are in

French (Biet). For Antigone, however, one has the excellent book of George Steiner, which has much also to say about Oedipus.

5 THE INWARD TURN: NINETEENTH AND TWENTIETH CENTURIES

It is not easy to orient oneself in the multiple histories (philosophy, art, literature, psychology, anthropology, folklore) of Oedipus in this period. The only book that approaches anything like an overview is the one you are holding in your hands. For drama, there are two good collections of English translations: one by Sanderson and Zimmerman, the other by Kallich, MacLeish and Schoenbohm. For the Sphinx, Willis Goth Regier's *Book of the Sphinx* contains a mass of lore, attractively presented. In *Freud and Oedipus*, Peter L. Rudnytsky provides a biographical account of Freud's discovery of the Oedipus Complex. To understand Freud's ideas, the best thing is to read Freud, and the *SE* (see Abbreviations) makes it easy to do. For syntheses of Freud's often disparate statements of key concepts, see J. Laplanche and J.-B. Pontalis, *The Language of Psycho-Analysis*. I did not discuss psychoanalysis after Freud, because, after him, it is no longer a matter of Oedipus reception but history of the psychoanalytic movement. For Oedipus in modern art since the Renaissance, Sara Harrington's webpage is indispensable: http://www.libraries.rutgers.edu/rul/rr_ gateway/research_guides/art/art_lib/oedipus_art.shtml. There exists no book-length study of this fascinating subject. The various nineteenth- and twentieth-century authors of Oedipus dramas have their own bibliographies and bodies of scholarship, which are fairly easy to locate.

Conceptual work on the Oedipus myth vastly proliferated in the twentieth century. It was hardly confined to psychoanalysis. I discussed what seemed to me the high points. Someone else might have included, for example, René Girard. A collection of his writings on Oedipus, *Oedipus Unbound: Selected Writings on Rivalry and Desire*, appeared in 2004. These writings show Girard's thought evolving toward the full-blown statement of his scapegoat theory in *Violence and the Sacred* in 1977 (originally published in French in 1972).

Oedipus as scapegoat also had a separate (whether or not indepen-dent, I do not know) beginning in the field of Classics in an article by the great French classicist, Jean-Pierre Vernant, which appeared in 1972, the same year as Girard's book, and then in English in 1977–78. In other conceptual work which I did not discuss, Julia Kristeva incorporates the scapegoat into her interpretation of Sophocles' two Oedipus plays in *Powers of Horror*, pp. 83–89.

WORKS CITED

Aarne, Antti. 1918–20. *Vergleichende Rätselforschungen*. FF Communications, 26–28. Helsinki: Academia Scientiarum Fennica.

Aarne, Antti and Stith Thompson. 1981. *The Types of the Folktale: A Classification and Bibliography*. 2nd ed. FF Communications, 184. Helsinki: Academia Scientiarum Fennica.

Abele, Wilhelm. 1899. *Die antiken Quellen des Hans Sachs*. Vol. 2. Beilage zum Programm der Realanstalt in Cannstatt zum Schlusse des Schuljahrs 1898/99. Cannstatt: Louis Bosheuyer.

Aélion, Rachel. 1986. *Quelques grands mythes héroïques dans l'oeuvre d'Euripide*. Paris: Les Belles Lettres.

Agamben, Giorgio. 1993. *Stanzas: Word and Phantasm in Western Culture*. Trans. by Ronald L. Martinez. Theory and History of Literature, 69. Minneapolis: University of Minnesota Press.

Anguillara, Giovanni Andrea dell'. 1809. *Teatro italiano antico*. Vol. 8. Milan: Società Tipografica de' Classici Italiani.

Anouilh, Jean. 1986. *Oedipe ou Le Roi boiteux d'après Sophocle*. Paris: La Table Ronde.

Astier, Colette. 1974. *Le mythe d'OEdipe*. Paris: Armand Colin.

Auerbach, Erich. [1946]1953. *Mimesis: The Representation of Reality in Western Literature*. Trans. by Willard R. Trask. Princeton: Princeton University Press. Orig. pub. Bern: A. Francke, 1946.

Avezzù, Guido, ed. 2003. *Il dramma sofocleo: Testo, lingua, interpretazione*. M & P Schriftenreihe für Wissenschaft und Forschung. Drama, 13. Stuttgart: Metzler.

Baswell, Christopher. 2000. "Marvels of Translation and Crises of Transition in the Romances of Antiquity." In R.L. Krueger, ed., *The Cambridge Companion to Medieval Romance*. Cambridge: Cambridge University Press. Pp. 29–44.

Benjamin, Walter. [1931–32]1966. *Ausgewählte Schriften*. Vol. 2. Die Bücher der Neunzehn, 78. Frankfurt am Main: Suhrkamp.

Berg, Stephen and Diskin Clay. 1978. *Oedipus the King*. New York: Oxford University Press.

Bettini, Maurizio and Giulio Guidorizzi. 2004. *Il mito di Edipo*. Turin: Einaudi.

Biet, Christian. 1994a. "Oedipe dans la tragédie du XVIIe siècle: Mémoire mythologique, mémoire juridique, mémoire généalogique." *Papers in French Seventeenth Century Literature* 21 (41): 499–518.

——. 1994b. *Oedipe en monarchie: tragédie et théorie juridique à l'âge classique*. Paris: Klincksieck.

——. 1999. "La fable d'Oedipe-Roi: de la démocratie grecque à la monarchie française." In Biet, ed., 1999: 26–47.

Biet, Christian, ed. 1999. *Oedipe*. Paris: Editions Autrement.

Blüher, Karl A. 1978. "Die spanische Literatur." In Lefèvre, ed., 1978: 132–72.

Blumenberg, Hans. 1985. *Work on Myth*. Trans. by Robert M. Wallace. Cambridge, MA: MIT Press.

Blumenfeld-Kosinski, Renate. 1997. *Reading Myth: Classical Mythology and its Interpretations in Medieval French Literature*. Stanford, CA: Stanford University Press.

Blundell, Ruby. 2002. *Sophocles: The Theban Plays: Antigone, King Oidipous, Oidipous at Colonus*. Newburyport, MA: Focus.

Bollack, Jean. 1990. *L'Oedipe roi de Sophocle: le texte et ses interprétations*. 4 vols. Cahiers de philologie, 11–13b. Villeneuve d'Ascq: Presses Universitaires de Lille.

Borza, Elia. 2003. "Sophocle et le XVIe Siècle." In Avezzù, ed., 2003: 49–58.

Braun, Richard Emil. 1973. *Antigone*. New York: Oxford University Press.

Breuer, Lee and Bob Telson. 1989. *The Gospel at Colonus*. New York: Theatre Communications Group.

Brown, Peter. 1967. *Augustine of Hippo: A Biography*. Berkeley: University of California Press.

Burian, Peter and Brian Swann. 1981. *The Phoenician Women*. New York: Oxford University Press.

Burkert, Walter. 1985. *Greek Religion*. Trans. by John Raffan. Cambridge, MA: Harvard University Press.

Buxton, R.G.A. 1980. "Blindness and Limits: Sophokles and the Logic of Myth." *Journal of Hellenic Studies* 100: 22–37.

Cameron, Alan. 2004. *Greek Mythography in the Roman World*. New York: Oxford University Press.

Campagne, Michèle, ed. 1989. *Oedipe / André Gide*. Catania: C.U.E.C.M.

Cavafy, Constantine. 1976. *The Complete Poems of Cavafy.* Trans. by Rae Dalven. New York: Harcourt Brace Jovanovich.

Cèbe, J.-P. 1990. *Varron, Satires Ménippées.* Vol. 9. Rome: École Française de Rome.

Chadwick, Whitney. 1975. "Eros or Thanatos – The Surrealist Cult of Love Reexamined." *Artforum* November: 46–56.

Charlton, H.B. [1921]1974. *The Senecan Tradition in Renaissance Tragedy: A Re-Issue of an Essay Published in 1921.* Folcroft, PA: Folcroft Library Editions.

Cherqui, Guy. 1989. "Une représentation du mythe: Oedipe résoud l'énigme du Sphinx de J.B. Ingres." *Studi di Letteratura Francese* 15: 207–19.

Cingano, Ettore. 1992. "The Death of Oedipus in the Epic Tradition." *Phoenix* 46: 1–11.

——. 2003a. "Figure eroiche nell' Antigone di Sofocle e nella tradizione mitografica arcaica." In Avezzù, ed., 2003: 69–84.

——. 2003b. "The Sacrificial Cut and the Sense of Honour Wronged in Greek Epic Poetry: *Thebais*, Frgs. 2–3D." In Cristiano Grottanelli and Lucio Milano, eds, *Food and Identity.* History of the Ancient Near East, 9. Padua: S.A.R.G.O.N.

Cixous, Hélène. 1978. *Le nom d'Oedipe: chant du corps interdit.* Paris: Éditions des Femmes.

Cocteau, Jean. 1952. *Gide vivant.* Paris: Amiot-Dumont.

——. 1956. *The Hand of a Stranger.* Trans. by Alec Brown. London: Elek Books.

——. 1959–1960. *Poésie critique.* 2 vols. Paris: Gallimard.

——. 1971. *La Machine infernale.* Ed. by W.M. Landers. London: Harrap.

——. 1991. "On an Oratorio." In John, ed., 1991: 21–27.

Coley, John S., trans. 1986. *Le Roman de Thèbes.* New York: Garland.

Collard, Christopher. 2005. "Euripidean Fragmentary Plays: The Nature of Sources and their Effect on Reconstruction." In Fiona McHardy, James Robson, and David Harvey, eds, *Lost Dramas of Classical Athens: Greek Tragic Fragments.* Exeter, UK: University of Exeter Press. Pp. 49–62.

Collard, Christopher, M.J. Cropp, and K.H. Lee, eds. 1995–2004. *Euripides: Selected Fragmentary Plays.* 2 vols. Warminster: Aris and Phillips.

Conradie, P.J. 1994. "The Gods are not to blame: Ola Rotimi's version of the Oedipus myth." *Akroterion* 39: 27–36.

Constans, Léopold E. 1890. *Le roman de Thèbes.* 2 vols. Paris: F. Didot.

Corneille, Pierre. 1987. *Oeuvres complètes.* Vol. 3. Ed. by Georges Couton. Paris: Gallimard.

Cunliffe, John W. 1906. *Supposes and Jocasta.* Boston: D.C. Heath.

Daly, James. 1990. *Horizontal Resonance as a Principle of Composition in the Plays of Sophocles.* New York: Garland.

Damsté, P.H. 1917. "Oedipus Indicus." *Mnemosyne* NS 45: 231–32.

Dawe, R.D., ed. 1996. *Sophocles, the Classical Heritage.* New York: Garland.

de Kock, E.L. 1961. "The Sophoklean Oidipus and Its Antecedents." *Acta Classica* 4: 7–28.

——. 1962. "The Peisandros Scholium – Its Sources, Unity, and Relationship to Euripides' *Chrysippus.*" *Acta Classica* 5: 15–37.

Deleuze, Gilles and Felix Guattari. 1983. *Anti-Oedipus: Capitalism and Schizophrenia.* Trans. by Robert Hurley, Mark Seem, and Helen R. Lane. Pref. by Michel Foucault. Minneapolis: University of Minnesota Press.

Devereux, George. 1973. "The self-blinding of Oidipous in Sophokles." *Journal of Hellenic Studies* 93: 36–49.

Dodds, E.R. 1966. "On Misunderstanding the Oedipus Rex." *G&R* 13: 37–49.

Edmunds, Lowell. 1981a. *The Sphinx in the Oedipus Legend.* Beiträge zur klassischen Philologie, 127. Königstein/Ts.: Anton Hain.

——. 1981b. "The Cults and the Legend of Oedipus." *Harvard Studies in Classical Philology* 85: 221–38. Repr. in Gregory Nagy, ed., *Greek Literature.* Vol. 4. Greek Literature in the Classical Period: The Poetics of Drama in Athens. London: Routledge, 2001.

——. 1982. "A Note on Boccaccio's Sources for the Story of Oedipus in *De casibus illustrium virorum.*" *Aevum* 16: 248–52.

——. 1985. *Oedipus: The Ancient Legend and its Later Analogues.* Baltimore: The Johns Hopkins University Press.

——. 1991. "Oedipus in the Twentieth Century: Principal Dates." *Classical and Modern Literature* 11: 317–24.

——. 1996. *Theatrical Space and Historical Place in Sophocles' Oedipus at Colonus.* Lanham, MD: Rowman and Littlefield.

——. 2000. "The Teiresias Scene in Sophocles' *Oedipus Tyrannus.*" *Syllecta Classica* 11: 33–73.

——. 2002. "Oedipus as Tyrant in Sophocles' *Oedipus Tyrannus or* Oedipus and Athens." *Syllecta Classica* 13: 63–103.

Ellenberger, Henri. 1970. *The Discovery of the Unconscious: The History and Evolution of Dynamic Psychiatry.* New York: Basic Books.

Erdmann, Axel and Eilert Ekwall, ed. 1930. *Lydgate's Siege of Thebes.* 2 vols. London: Early English Text Society.

Farrell, Joseph. 2001. *Latin Language and Latin Culture: From Ancient to Modern Times.* Cambridge: Cambridge University Press.

Fitch, John G. 2002–4. *Seneca: Tragedies.* 2 vols. Loeb Classical Library. Cambridge, MA: Harvard University Press.

Flashar, Hellmut. 1991. *Inszenierung der Antike: Das griechische Drama auf der Bühne der Neuzeit, 1585–1990.* Munich: C.H. Beck.

——. 1996. "Hegel, Oedipus and die Tragödie." In Christoph Jamme, ed., *Kunst und Geschichte im Zeitalter Hegels*. Hamburg: F. Meiner. Pp. 1–25.

——. 2001. *Felix Mendelssohn-Bartholdy und die griechische Tragödie: Bühnenmusik im Kontext von Politik, Kultur und Bildung*. Leipzig: Verlag der Sächsischen Akademie der Wissenschaften zu Leipzig.

Fontenrose, Joseph. 1978. *The Delphic Oracle: Its Responses and Operations, With a Catalogue of Responses*. Berkeley: University of California Press.

Fraser, Donald. 1914. *Winning a Primitive People*. London: Seley.

Frick, Werner. 1998. *"Die mythische Methode": Komparatistische Studien zur Transformation der griechischen Tragödie im Drama der klassischen Moderne*. Tübingen: Niemeyer.

Gallo, Alberto. 1973. *La prima rappresentazione al Teatro Olimpico con i progetti e le relazioni dei contemporanei*. Milan: Il polifilo.

Gantz, Timothy. 1993. *Early Greek Myth: A Guide to the Literary and Artistic Sources*. Baltimore: The Johns Hopkins University Press.

Garin, E. 1973. "La diffusione della Poetica di Aristotele dal secolo XV in poi." *RCSF* 28: 447–51.

Garland, Robert. 2004. *Surviving Greek Tragedy*. London: Duckworth.

Gide, André. 1948. *Journals*. 4 vols. Trans. by Justin O'Brien. New York: Knopf.

——. 1950. *Two Legends: Oedipus and Theseus*. Trans. by John Russell. New York: Knopf.

Girard, René. 1977. *Violence and the Sacred*. Baltimore: The Johns Hopkins University Press.

——. 2004. *Oedipus Unbound: Selected Writings on Rivalry and Desire*. Ed. by Mark Anspach. Stanford, CA: Stanford University Press.

Gordon, D.J. 1975. "Academicians Build a Theater and Give a Play." In Stephen Orgel, ed., *The Renaissance Imagination*. Berkeley: University of California Press. Pp. 246–65.

Goux, Jean-Joseph. 1992. *Oedipe philosophe*. Paris: Aubier.

——. 1993. *Oedipus, Philosopher*. Trans. by Catherine Porter. Stanford, CA: Stanford University Press.

Grennan, Eamon and Rachel Kitzinger. 2005. *Oedipus at Colonus*. New York: Oxford University Press.

Griffith, Mark. 1999. *Sophocles: Antigone*. Cambridge: Cambridge University Press.

Grout, Patricia. 1977. "Religion and Mythology in the *Roman de Thèbes*." In H.T. Barnwell, ed., *The Classical Tradition in French Literature: Essays Presented to R.C. Knight by Colleagues, Pupils and Friends*. London: Grant and Cutler. Pp. 23–39.

Guffey, George R. and Alan Roper, eds. 1984. *The Works of John Dryden*. Vol. 13. Berkeley: University of California Press.

Hain, Mathilde. 1966. *Rätsel*. Metzler: Stuttgart.

Halm-Tisserant, Monique. 1981. "La sphinx amoreuse: un schéma Grec dans l'oeuvre de G. Moreau." *Revue des Archaeologues et Historiens d'Art de Louvain* 14: 30–70.

Halperin, David M. 1990. *One Hundred Years of Homosexuality*. New York: Routledge.

——. 1996. "Homosexuality." In Simon Hornblower and Anthony Spawforth, eds, *The Oxford Classical Dictionary*. 3rd ed. Oxford: Oxford University Press.

Hart, Donn V. 1964. *Riddles in Filipino Folklore: An Anthropological Analysis*. Syracuse: Syracuse University Press.

Hecht, Anthony and Helen Bacon. 1973. *Seven against Thebes*. New York: Oxford University Press.

Hederer, Edgar. 1960. *Hugo von Hofmansthal*. Frankfurt am Main: S. Fischer.

Hegel, Georg W.F. 1975. *Aesthetics: Lectures on Fine Art*. Trans. by T.M. Knox. 2 vols. Oxford: Clarendon Press.

——. 1987. *Lectures on the Philosophy of Religion*. Vol. 2. Trans. by J. Michael Stewart *et al*. Berkeley: University of California Press.

Heidegger, Martin. [1953]1961. *An Introduction to Metaphysics*. Trans. by Ralph Manheim. Garden City, NY: Doubleday and Co. Orig. pub. by Yale University Press, 1959; repr. 1984. Trans. of *Einführung in die Metaphysik*. Tübingen: Max Niemeyer, 1953.

Heinrich, Klaus. 1993. *Dahlemer Vorlesungen*. Vol. 3 ("arbeiten mit ödipus: Begriff der Verdrängung in der Religionswissenschaft"). Ed. by H.-A. Kücken, Wolfgang Albrecht, and Irene Tobben. Basel: Stroemfeld.

Hofmannsthal, Hugo von. 1983. *Sämtliche Werke*. Vol. 8. Ed. by Wolfgang Nehring and K.E. Bohnenkamp. Frankfurt am Main: S. Fischer.

Hölderlin, Friedrich. 1994. *Friedrich Hölderlin: Sämtliche Werke und Briefe*. Vol. 2. Ed. by Jochen Schmidt. Frankfurt am Main: Deutscher Klassiker.

——. 2001. *Hölderlin's Sophocles: Oedipus and Antigone*. Trans. by David Constantine. Highgreen, UK: Bloodaxe.

Holland, Eugene W. 1999. *Deleuze and Guattari's Anti-Oedipus: Introduction to Schizoanalysis*. London: Routledge.

Holthusen, Hans E. 1960. "Was ist abendländisch? Fünf Leitfiguren europäischen Literatur." *Merkur* 14: 605–24.

Hughes, Ted. 2003. *Collected Poems*. Ed. by Paul Keegan. New York: Farrar, Straus and Giroux.

Hutchinson, G.O., ed. 1985. *Aeschylus: Septem contra Thebas*. Oxford: Clarendon Press.

Hutton, James. 1982. *Aristotle's Poetics*. New York: Norton.

Jebb, R.C. 1893. *Sophocles: The Plays and Fragments. Part I. The Oedipus Tyrannus*. 3rd ed. Cambridge: Cambridge University Press. Repr. Adolf M. Hakkert: Amsterdam, 1966. Repr. with intro. by Jeffrey Rusten. London: Bristol Classical Press, 2004.

John, Nicholas, ed. 1991. *Oedipus Rex; the Rake's Progress*. English National Opera Guides, 43. London: John Calder. Pp. 7–43.

Kallich, Martin, Andrew MacLeish, and Gertrude Schoenbohm, eds. 1968. *Oedipus: Myth and Drama*. New York: Odyssey Press.

Katz, Joshua. Forthcoming. "The Riddle of the *sp(h)ij-*: The Greek Sphinx and her Indic and Indo-European Background." In Pinault, Georges-Jean and Daniel Petit, eds, *La Langue poétique indo-européenne*. Leuven: Peeters,

Kearns, Emily. 1989. *The Heroes of Attica*. London: University of London, Institute of Classical Studies.

Keller, Adelbert von, ed. 1874. *Hans Sachs*. Vol. 8. Tübingen: Der Literarische Verein in Stuttgart. Repr. Hildesheim: Olms, 1964.

Keller, Adelbert von and Edmund Goetze, eds. 1892. *Hans Sachs*. Vol. 20. Tübingen: Der Literarische Verein in Stuttgart. Repr. Hildesheim: Olms, 1964.

Kocziszky, Éva. 1995. "'Wenn einer in den Spiegel siehet': Hölderlin und das Oedipus-Drama." *Recherches germaniqes* 25: 133–58.

Kovacs, David. 1994–2002. *Euripides*. 6 vols. Loeb Classical Library. Cambridge, MA: Harvard University Press.

Krauskopf, Ingrid. 1974. *Der thebanische Sagenkreis und andere griechische Sagen in der etruskischen Kunst*. Schriften zur antiken Mythologie, 2. Mainz: Heidelberger Akademie der Wissenschaften.

——. 1994. "Oidipous." In John Boardman *et al.*, ed., *Lexicon Iconographicum Mythologiae Classicae*. Vol. 7.1. Zurich: Artemis.

Kreuzer, Bettina. 1992. *Frühe Zeichner, 1500–500 vor Chr.: Aegyptische, griechische und etruskische Vasenfragmente der Sammlung H. A. Cahn, Basel*. Freiburg i. Br.: Freundeskreis der Archäologischen Sammlung der Universität Freiburg i. Br. Pp. 86–88.

Kristeva, Julia. 1982. *Powers of Horror*. Trans. by Leon Roudiez. New York: Columbia University Press.

Kurzweil, Edith. 1995. *Freudians and Feminists*. Boulder: Westview.

Laplanche, J. and J.-B. Pontalis. 1973. *The Language of Psycho-Analysis*. Trans. by Donald Nicholson-Smith. London: Hogarth Press.

Lear, Jonathan. 1998. *Open Minded: Working Out the Logic of the Soul*. Cambridge, MA: Harvard University Press.

Lefèvre, Eckard, ed. 1978. *Der Einfluss Senecas auf das europaische Drama*. Darmstadt: Wissenschaftliche Buchgesellschaft.

Lévi-Strauss, Claude. [1955]1967. "The Structural Study of Myth." In *Structural Anthropology*. Garden City, NY: Doubleday. Pp. 202–28. This article was orig. pub. in *Journal of American Folkore* 68 (1955): 428–44.

——. [1973]1976. *Structural Anthropology*. Vol. 2. Trans. by Monique Layton. Chicago: University of Chicago Press.

——. [1985]1988. *The Jealous Potter*. Trans. by Bénédicte Chorier. Chicago: University of Chicago Press. Trans. of *La potière jalouse*, Paris: Plon, 1985.

Lloyd-Jones, Hugh. 1983. *The Justice of Zeus*. 2nd ed. Berkeley: University of California Press.

——. 1996. *Sophocles: Fragments*. Loeb Classical Library. Cambridge, MA: Harvard University Press.

——. 2002. "Curses and Divine Anger in Early Greek Epic: The Pisander Scholion." *CQ* 52: 1–14.

Lloyd-Jones, Hugh and N.G. Wilson. 1990. *Sophoclea: Studies on the Text of Sophocles*. Oxford: Clarendon Press.

Malcolm, Janet. 1984. *In the Freud Archives*. New York: Knopf.

Malcolm, Noel. 1990. *George Enescu: His Life and Music*. London: Toccata Press.

Mann, Nicholas. 1996. "The Origins of Humanism." In Jill Kraye, ed., *The Cambridge Companion to Renaissance Humanism*. Cambridge: Cambridge University Press. Pp. 1–19.

Martin, Richard. 2003. *Myths of the Ancient Greeks*. New York: New American Library.

Masson, Jeffrey. 1985. *The Assault on Truth: Freud's Suppression of the Seduction Theory*. New York: Penguin Books.

Mastrocola, Paola. 1996. *Nimica fortuna: Edipo e Antigone nella tragedia italiana del Cinquecento*. Turin: Tirrenia.

Melanchthon, Philipp. 1834–60. *Philippi Melanthonis Opera quae supersunt omnia*. Ed. by C.G. Bretschneider. 28 vols. Halle: C.A. Schwetschke.

Messerli, Sylviane. 2002. *Oedipe entenébré: Legendes d'Oedipe au XII siècle*. Paris: Champion.

Miller, Frank J. 1917. *Seneca's Tragedies*. 2 vols. Cambridge, MA: Harvard University Press.

Moret, Jean-Marc. 1984. *Oedipe, la Sphinx, et les Thébains*. 2 vols. Geneva: Institut Suisse de Rome.

Nagy, Gregory. [1979]1999. *The Best of the Achaeans: Concepts of the Hero in Archaic Greek Poetry*. Rev. ed. Baltimore: The Johns Hopkins University Press.

Nice, David. 1991. "The Person of Fate and the Fate of the Person: Stravinsky's 'Oedipus Rex'." In John, ed. 1991: 7–15.

Nietzsche, Friedrich Wilhelm. [1872]2000. *The Birth of Tragedy*. Trans. by Douglas Smith. Oxford: Oxford University Press.

Nussbaum, Daniel. 1994. *PL8SPK: California Vanity Plates Retell the Classics*. New York: HarperCollinsWest.

Odagiri, Mitsutaka. 2001. *Écritures palimpsestes, ou, Les théâtralisations françaises du mythe d'Oedipe*. Paris: L'Harmattan.

Ohly, Freidrich. [1976]1992. *The Damned and the Elect: Guilt in Western Culture*. Trans. by Linda Archibald. Cambridge: Cambridge University Press. Orig. pub. as *Der Verfluchte und der Erwählte: Vom Leben mit der Schuld*. Vorträge: Rheinisch-Westfälische Akademie der Wissenschaften, G 207. Opladen: Westdeutscher Verlag, 1976.

Osborn, Max. 1893. *Die Teufelliteratur des XVI. Jahrhunderts*. Acta Germanica 3.3. Berlin: Mayer and Müller.

Paduano, Guido. 1994. *Lunga storia di Edipo Re: Freud, Sofocle e il teatro occidentale*. Turin: Einaudi.

Palmer, Anne-Marie. 1989. *Prudentius on the Martyrs*. Oxford: Clarendon Press.

Parsons, P.J. 1999. "30–37 Epigram IV: the Sphinx unriddled." In N. Gonis *et al.* ed., *The Oxyrhynchus Papyri* 66. London: Egyptian Exploration Society. Pp. 43–49, 53–55.

Pasolini, Pier Paolo. 1971. *Oedipus Rex: A Film*. Trans. by John Mathews. London: Lorrimer Publishing.

Pavese, Cesare. 1965. *Dialogues witih Leucò*. Trans. by William Arrowsmith and D.S. Carne-Ross. Ann Arbor: University of Michigan Press. Trans. of *Dialoghi con Leucò*. Turin: Einaudi, 1953.

Péladan, Joséphin. 1903. *Oedipe et le Sphinx*. 4th ed. Paris: Société du Mercure de France.

Porzig, Walter. 1953. "Das Rätsel der Sphinx." *Lexis* 3: 236–39. Repr. in R. Schmitt, ed., *Indogermanische Dichtersprache*. Darmstadt: Wissenschaftliche Buchgesellschaft, 1968. Pp. 172–76.

Posèq, Avigdor W.G. 2001. "Ingres's Oedipal Oedipus and the Sphinx." *Notes in the History of Art* 21.1: 24–32.

Praz, Mario. 1967. *The Romantic Agony*. 2nd ed. New York: Meridian Books.

Propp, Vladimir. [1928]1968. *Morphology of the Folktale*. Trans. by Laurence Scott. 2nd ed. Austin: University of Texas Press.

——. [1944]1983. "Oedipus in the Light of Folklore." In Lowell Edmunds and Alan Dundes, ed., *Oedipus: A Folklore Casebook*. New York: Garland. Pp. 76–121. Orig. pub. in *Ucenye zapiski Leningradskogo gosudarsivennogo universiteta*, Serija filologiceskich 72, fasc. 9, pp. 138–75.

——. [1946]1983. *Les racines historiques du conte merveilleux*. Trans. by Lise

Gruel-Apert. Paris: Gallimard. Orig. pub. as *Istoricheskie korni volshebnoi skazki*. Leningrad: Priboi 1946).

——. 1984. *Theory and History of Folklore*. Ed. by Anatoly Liberman. Trans. by Ariadna Y. Martin, Richard P. Martin *et al*. Theory and history of literature, 5. Minneapolis: University of Minnesota Press.

Punzi, Arianna. 1995. *Oedipodae confusa domus: La materia tebana nel Medioevo latino e romanzo*. Rome: Bagatti.

Rank, Otto. [1912]1992. *The Incest Theme in Literature and Legend: Fundamentals of a Psychology of Literary Creation*. Trans. by Gregory C. Richter; with an introductory essay by Peter Rudnytsky. Baltimore: The Johns Hopkins University Press. Trans. of *Das Inzest-motiv in Dichtung und Sage*. Leipzig: F. Deuticke, 1912.

Regier, Willis Goth. 2004. *Book of the Sphinx*. Lincoln: University of Nebraska Press.

Reid, Jane Davidson. 1993. *The Oxford Guide to Classical Mythology in the Arts, 1300–1990s*. 2 vols. New York: Oxford University Press.

Reynolds, L.D., ed. 1983. *Texts and Transmission: A Survey of the Latin Classics*. Oxford: Clarendon Press.

Reynolds, L.D. and N.G. Wilson. 1991. *Scribes and Scholars: A Guide to the Transmission of Greek and Latin Literature*. 3rd ed. Oxford: Clarendon Press.

Riccoboni, Antonio. 1996. "Letter Describing the Performance of *Oedipus Rex* at Vicenza in 1585." In Dawe, ed., 1996: 1–12.

Robert, Carl. 1915. *Oidipus; Geschichte eines poetischen Stoffs im grieschen Altertum*. 2 vols. Berlin: Weidmann.

Róheim, Géza. 1934. *The Riddle of the Sphinx, or Human Origins*. Trans. by R. Money-Kyrle. London: Hogarth Press.

Rokem, Freddie. 1996. "One Voice and Many Legs: Oedipus and the Riddle of the Sphinx." In Galit Hasan-Rokem and David Shulman, eds, *Untying the Knot*. New York: Oxford University Press. Pp. 255–70.

Rösch-von der Heyde, Wiebke. 1999. *Das Sphinx-Bild im Wandel der Zeiten: Vorkommen und Bedeutung*. Rahden: Marie Leidord.

Rubin, James H. 1973. "Oedipus, Antigone and Exiles in Post-Revolutionary French Painting." *Art Quarterly* 36: 141–71.

——. 1979. "Ingres' Vision of Oedipus and the Sphinx: The Riddle Resolved?" *Arts Magazine* 54 (2): 130–33.

Rudnytsky, Peter L. 1987. *Freud and Oedipus*. New York: Columbia University Press.

Sachs, Hans. 1884. *Hans Sachs' Werke*. Ed. by Dr. Arnold. Vol. 20. Deutsche National-Litteratur. Berlin and Stuttgart: W. Spemann. Repr. Tübingen: Max Niemeyer, 1974.

Sanderson, James L. and Zimmerman, eds. 1968. *Oedipus Myth and Dramatic Form*. Boston: Houghton Mifflin.

Sandys, John E. 1906–8. *A History of Classical Scholarship*. 3 vols. Cambridge: Cambridge University Press.

Saunders, Glen. 1996. "Qu Xiaosong's Opera the Death of Oedipus: A Chinese Composer's views on Greek Drama and Buddhism." *Chime: Newsletter of the European Foundation for Chinese Music Research = Ch'ing* 9: 46–56.

Schadewalt, Wolfgang. 1996. "Hölderlin's Translations." In Dawe, ed., 1996: 101–10.

Schlegel, August Wilhelm. 1846. *A Course of Lectures on Dramatic Art and Literature*. Trans. by John Black. London: H.G. Bohn. pp. 96–110.

——. [1846]1996. "Life and Political Character of Sophocles – Character of His Different Tragedies." In Dawe, ed., 1996: 159–70.

Schmidt, Peter L. 1978. "Rezeption und Überlieferung bis Ausgang des Mittelalters." In Lefèvre, ed., 1978: 12–73.

Schrade, Leo. 1960. *La représentation d'Edipo Tirano au Teatro Olimpico (Vicence 1585)*. Paris: Centre National de la Recherche Scientifique.

Schultz, Wolfgang. 1914. "Rätsel." In A. Pauly, G. Wissowa, and W. Kroll, eds, *Real-Encyclopädie der klassischen Altertumswissenschaft*. 2nd series. Vol. 1. Stuttgart: Metzler. Cols. pp. 69–70.

Segal, Charles. 2001. *Oedipus Tyrannus: Tragic Heroism and the Limits of Knowledge*. 2nd ed. New York: Oxford University Press.

Seidensticker, Bernd. 1972. "Beziehungen zwischen den beiden Oidipusdramen des Sophokles." *Hermes* 100: 255–74.

Shackleton Bailey, D.R. 2003. *Statius: Thebaid*. 2 vols. Loeb Classical Library. Cambridge, MA: Harvard University Press.

Smollett, Tobias. 1901. *The Works of Voltaire*. 41 vols. Volumes 8–9: The dramatic works of Voltaire. Paris: E.R. Du Mont. Repr. in Sanderson and Zimmerman, eds, 1968: 105–43.

Smyth, H.W. 1963. *Aeschylus*. Vol. 2. With an appendix of fragments ed. by Hugh Lloyd-Jones. Cambridge, MA: Harvard University Press.

Steiner, George. 1986. *Antigones*. Oxford: Clarendon Press.

Stravinsky, Igor. 1936. *Stravinsky: An Autobiography*. New York: Simon and Schuster.

Stravinsky, Igor and Robert Craft. 1963. *Dialogues and a Diary*. Garden City, NY: Doubleday.

Theile, Wolfgang. 1975. "Stoffgeschichte und Poetik – Literarischer Vergleich von Ödipus-Dramen (Sophokles, Corneille, Gide)." *Arcadia* 10: 34–51.

Tigerstedt, E.N. 1968. "Observations on the Reception of Aristotle's 'Poetics' in the Latin West." *Studies in the Renaissance* 15: 7–24.

Tschiedel, Hans Jürgen. 1978. "Die italienische Literatur." In Lefèvre, ed., 1978: 74–131.

Uerscheln, Gabriele. 1993. "Anmerkungen zu Gustave Moreaus 'Le Sphinx Vainqueur.'" *Neusser Jahrbuch für Kunst, Kulturgeschichte und Heimatkunde*: 31–36.

Ventris, Michael and John Chadwick. 1956. *Documents in Mycenaean Greek*. Cambridge: Cambridge University Press.

Vernant, Jean-Pierre. 1977–78. "Ambiguity and Reversal: On the Enigmatic Structure of *Oedipus Rex*." *New Literary History* 9: 475–501.

Vessey, D.W.T.C. 1982. "Flavian epic." In E.J. Kenney and W.V. Clausen, eds, *The Cambridge History of Classical Literature*. Vol. II, *Latin Literature*. Cambridge: Cambridge University Press. Pp. 558–96.

Vidal-Naquet, Pierre. 1981. "Oedipe à Vicenne et à Paris." *Quaderni di Storia* 14: 3–29. Trans. as Vidal-Naquet, 1996.

——. 1996. "Oedipus at Vicenza and at Paris: Two Stages in a Saga." In Dawe, ed., 1996: 13–31.

Vitz, P.C. and J. Gartner. 1984. "Christianity and Psychoanalysis. Part 1: Jesus as the Anti-Oedipus." *Journal of Psychology and Theology* 12: 4–14.

Voltaire (Arouet, François-Marie). 1820. *Oeuvres complètes*. Vol. 2. Paris: E.A. Lequien.

von Platen, August Graf. 1895. *August Graf von Platens sämtliche Werke*. Vol. 10. Ed. by Max Koch. Leipzig: Hesse and Bekker.

Wagner, Richard. [1868]1913. *Opera and Drama*. 2 vols. Trans. by Edwin Evans. London: William Reeves.

Walsh, Stephen. 1993. *Stravinsky: Oedipus Rex*. Cambridge: Cambridge University Press.

Wanke, Christiane. 1978. "Die französische Literatur." In Lefèvre, ed., 1978: 173–234.

Wat, Pierre and Patrick Absalon. 1999. ""«Oedipus Fecit» ou peut-on voir Œdipe en peinture?" In Biet, ed., 1999: 90–98.

Weinberg, Bernard. 1961. *A History of Literary Criticism in the Italian Renaissance*. 2 vols. Chicago: University of Chicago Press.

Weir, Judith. 1991. "'Oedipus Rex': A Personal View." In John, ed., 1991: 17–20.

ABBREVIATIONS

Aesch. = Aeschylus

Ant. = Antigone

Anth. Pal. = Palatine Anthology

AT = Aarne-Thompson = Aarne, Antti and Stith Thompson. *The Types of the Folktale: A Classification and Bibliography.* 2nd ed. FF Communications 184. Helsinki: Academia Scientiarum Fennica, 1981.

Athenaeus = Athenaeus, *The Deipnosophists* or *The Learned Banquet*

Austin = Colin Austin, ed., *Nova Fragmenta Euripidea in Papyris Reperta.* Berlin: de Gruyter, 1968.

Bacch. = Bacchae

Bernabé = Albertus Bernabé, ed., *Poetarum epicorum Graecorum: testimonia et fragmenta.* Leipzig: Teubner, 1987.

Davies = Malcolm Davies, ed., *Epicorum Graecorum fragmenta.* Göttingen: Vandenhoeck & Ruprecht, 1988. Or Malcolm Davies, ed., *Poetarum Melicorum Graecorum Fragmenta*, vol. 1. Oxford: Clarendon Press, 1991.

Eur. = Euripides

F = fragment in references to *FGrH*

FGrH = Felix Jacoby, *Die Fragmente der griechischen Historiker*, in many vols. Leiden: Brill, 1923– .

fr. = fragment

Hdt. = Herodotus

Hes. = Hesiod

Il. = Iliad

jul = *Divus Julius*

Kannicht = Richard Kannicht, ed., *Euripides*, in *Tragicorum graecorum fragmenta*, vol. 5. Göttingen: Vandenhoeck & Ruprecht, 2004.

Loeb = M.L. West, *Greek Epic Fragments*, Loeb Classical Library. Cambridge, MA: Harvard University Press, 2003.

Met. = *Metamorphoses*

M-W = Reinhold Merkelbach and M.L. West, *Fragmenta Hesiodea*. Oxford: Clarendon Press, 1967.

Od. = *Odyssey*

Or. = *Orestes*

Paus. = Pausanias

Phoen. = *Phoenician Women*

PMG = D.L. Page, ed., *Poetae Melici Graecae*. Oxford: Clarendon Press, 1962.

Radt = Stefan Radt, ed., *Aeschylus*, in *Tragicorum graecorum fragmenta*, vol. 3. Göttingen: Vandenhoeck & Ruprecht, 1985.

schol. Pind. *Ol.* = ancient scholiast on Pindar

SE = Sigmund Freud, *The Standard Edition of the Complete Psychological Works of Sigmund Freud*, trans. under the general editorship of James Strachey. London: Hogarth Press, 1953–74.

Sept. = *Septem contra Thebas* = *Seven Against Thebes*

Snell = Bruno Snell, ed., *Didascaliae tragicae*, etc., in *Tragicorum graecorum fragmenta*, vol. 1. Göttingen: Vandenhoeck & Ruprecht, 1971.

Snell-Kannicht = Bruno Snell and Richard Kannicht, ed., *Tragicorum graecorum fragmenta*, vol. 2. Göttingen: Vandenhoeck & Ruprecht, 1981.

Soph. = Sophocles

Stat. = Statius

Theb. = *Thebaid*

Theog. = *Theogony*

W^2 = M.L. West, ed., *Iambi et Elegi Graeci*, 2nd ed. (2 vols. in 1). Oxford: Clarendon Press, 1989–92.

INDEX

Page references in *italics* refer to illustrations.

Eurydice 93–95
Euryganeia 16, 20, 25–26, 39
exile 25, 39, 42–43, 50–53, 61–62, 104
eyewitness to murder of Laius 47–48

Fall of Princes (Lydgate) 71–72
Famous women (Boccaccio) 71, 88
fate 49–50, 61, 103, 112–13, 115
folktales 5–6, 74, 76–78, 121
'foot' motif 9, 44–46, 66, *66, 68,* 71,
 74, 114, 124
Frazer, J. G. 121
free will 103, 120
Freud, Sigmund 3–4, 7–8, 113–16,
 121–22, 130–31, 137–38
Frogs (Aristophanes) 49
funeral rites 21, 53

Gascoigne, George 86–87
Genealogie (Boccaccio) 65, 71
genealogies 13, 17, 21, 25, 54, 132
generations, multiple 13, 35, 37–39,
 44, 54, 59
ghost of Laius 62, 91, 94–96, 119
Gide, André 66, 116, 120–21, 131–32
Giocasta (Dolce) 86–87
Giotto 78
Gods Are Not to Blame, The (Rotimi)
 139–41
Golden Bough, The (Frazer) 121
Gospel at Colonus, The (Breuer and
 Telson) 8, 139
Goux, Jean-Joseph 127, 137, 139
Graham, Martha 132–35
graves of Oedipus 27–28, 37
Greek language, knowledge of 64, 83
Gregory legend 66, 76, 78, 129
Guattari, Felix 131

Haemon 17, 38–39, 54, 90, 94–95

'Hamlet and Oedipus' (Jones) 119
'hanging' motif 66, *66,* 71
Hegel, Friedrich 101–104, 125–27,
 129, 137
Heinrich, Klaus 126, 137
hero cult of Oedipus 26–30, 53
Hesiod 14, 17, 21–22, 26
historicization 121, 138
Hofmannsthal, Hugo von 112–13,
 139
Hölderlin, Friedrich 49, 100–101,
 112, 127
Homer 4, 13–17, 20–21, 24, 26, 28,
 41–42, 44
hubris (hybris) 49, 127
Hughes, Ted 10, 138
human and divine levels 24, 35, 37,
 91, 101, 103, 118
humanists 85–86
Hyperion (Hölderlin) 112

Ibycus 14–15
identity, search for 40–41, 46–47
ignorance 17, 41, 45, 102–103
Iliad (Homer) 14–15, 17, 21, 24, 42,
 44
incest 17, 20, 73, 94, 113–15, 124–25
incoherence 139–40
individualism 105–6, 120
inference 16–17, 34, 130
Infernal Machine, The (Cocteau)
 117–19, 135
Ingres, Jean-Auguste-Dominique
 102, 106–7, *108,* 126
Interpretation of Dreams, The
 (Freud) 113, 136
Iokasta (Enckell) 135
Ismene 51–52, 54, 69

Jealous Potter, The (Lévi-Strauss) 122

Related titles from Routledge

Dionysos

Richard Seaford

Dionysos is our oldest living symbol. First mentioned in texts of about 1200 BC, he was for the ancient Greeks the divine embodiment of wine, of mystery-cult, and of the theatre, and even today is valued as a symbol of something fundamental to being human. With the power of his epiphany Dionysos broke down the barriers of individual consciousness, he merged the individual into the group. He did it not only by wine, but also in the transformation of individuals in the theatre, and in the rehearsal of death in mystery-cult. In this way Dionysos could embody the whole community, but could also be a refined philosophical symbol.

He was the most serious rival to the spread of Christianity, by which he was not entirely eliminated: his resurgences in Renaissance Italy and nineteenth-century Germany are described in the final chapter of this book. *Dionysos*, a groundbreaking survey of one of the most enduring of Greek gods provides an excellent reference point for study and will also be of interest to readers in related disciplines.

ISBN10: 0–415–32487–4 (hbk)
ISBN10: 0–415–32488–2 (pbk)

ISBN13: 978–0–415–32487–8 (hbk)
ISBN13: 978–0–415–32488–5 (pbk)